TRAILER OWNERS HANDBOOK

A GUIDE FOR TRAILER AND TOW VEHICLE SELECTION, EQUIPAGE, MAINTENANCE, AND OPERATION.

BY ~~LCDR~~ JESSE J. DIPBOYE, ~~USN RET~~

All rights reserved including the rights of reproduction in whole or in part in any form.

COPYRIGHT, 1969, BY JESSE J. DIPBOYE

Library of Congress Catalog Number: 75-75469

Standard Book Number: 87593-091-3

PUBLISHED BY
Trail-R-Club of America

America's Largest Publisher of Books
Pertaining to Recreational Vehicles
and Mobile Home Living

Box 1376   Beverly Hills, California 90213

PRINTED IN THE UNITED STATES OF AMERICA

FOREWORD

It is hoped that the title of this book will not be misleading. Although some portions apply specifically to the 1965 and '67 Airstream, as those are the models the author towed during the more than two years during which material for the book was generated, most of the contents will apply in whole or in part to the towing or maintenance of other travel trailers. Therefore, it is felt that the title should be broad enough to attract the attention of **all** travel trailer neophytes, as there is much here that can be helpful and nothing (I believe) that can do any harm. It is hoped that this book will fill a part of the long recognized need for information that any travel trailer novice encounters when he takes up trailering.

Included herein is the information contained in my magazine articles "Preparing for the Alaska Highway" and "Add a Second Battery — and Relax", published in 1966 by Trailer Life Magazine.

Most manufacturers provide information through their dealers, some more than others. And some provide a fairly comprehensive owner's manual. However, even the best attempts in this respect are woefully inadequate for the new owner who is wholly inexperienced but intends to really travel — to get off the beaten path where he will be a long way from established trailer maintenance facilities — to travel to the wilderness parks, thru wastelands, to Alaska via the ALCAN Highway, to Mexico or Central America, thru the Western Rockies. Such a man needs the benefit of miles and miles of towing, under all kinds of conditions and over every type of terrain — and even the few dealers who have the know how can't afford the many hours that would be required to pass it along to the new owner. Hence this book. Any new owner needs more information than he is likely to get from his dealer or can be put in a trailer owner's manual, but the man who intends to venture needs it more and needs more of it.

The sad fact is that many dealers know next to nothing about the use of their products — some of them outlets for the leading makes. Many have never towed a trailer around the block, much less shaken one down on an extended caravan or travelled the mountains and deserts.

Manufacturers have for years concentrated their efforts on producing a more attractive package and boosting sales, to the neglect of servicing capability. Until Airstream inaugurated their "Certified Service Center" program in 1966 no manufacturer had, so far as I know, made any attempt to provide warranty service, or other repair service, anywhere except at the factory. Their service centers are authorized to repair not only the Airstream components, but appliances as well. As the service is newly established it has some growing pains, but most centers are well manned and are quite effective. It is only a matter of time until all major manufacturers will be forced, by customer demand, to come to the same solution.

It should be admitted here and now that the solutions offered herein may not always be the best possible. But they are the best I have, and they are unquestionably better than none at all — which is what the novice usually encounters at the outset. If some of you old hands pick this book up by mistake, and you have criticisms you don't think can go unheard — write a better book! This book wasn't written for you, anyway.

TABLE OF CONTENTS

FORWARD	1
SELECTING YOUR TRAVEL TRAILER	5
UNIT HARMONY	13
OTHER SAFETY AND RELIABILITY FACTORS	37
LEVELLING AND HOOKING UP	47
PREPARING FOR THE ROAD	61
RECOMMENDED DRIVING TECHNIQUES FOR TOWING TRAILERS	73
MAINTENANCE AND REPAIR	85
TOWING OVER UNPAVED ROADS	103
HOUSEKEEPING HINTS	109
GETTING THE MOST FROM YOUR TRAILER	115

Chapter 1

SELECTING YOUR TRAVEL TRAILER

Depending upon the use to which you expect to put your travel trailer, its selection can depend on only a few, or on a great many factors. As this book is meant primarily for those who want to travel anywhere and everywhere rather than for the "weekender", the treatment given here shall be aimed in that direction. In short, as many as possible of all the factors will be covered. There is always the chance that, once you have the capability in tow, your horizons may broaden.

Some of the questions you should ask before you venture out on "travel trailer row" are:

How many people must the trailer accommodate?

How much are you prepared to pay? For initial outlay? On an annual (replacement) basis? The latter is largely concerned with depreciation.

Will it be used year-round or only occasionally?

Will it be towed long distances, for prolonged vacations, where there may be need for maintaining relatively high cruising speeds, or only for short week-end trips?

Must it be intrinsically attractive, or is it intended merely to provide travel and lodging?

Must it have a water storage tank, with water under pressure?

Must it have a storage battery electrical system?

Must the electrical system be chargeable from the tow vehicle, to enable its use on long trips where no other electrical source is likely to be available?

Must it have a "sanitator" (sewage holding tank) or will it always be parked near public restrooms (state and Federal parks, etc.)? Even if the latter is the case you may be disinclined to use public facilities.

Must it have a heating system — and is there a requirement that the heating system be a circulatory system, providing evenly distributed heat throughout the trailer?

Will it be operated in hot weather — hence have need of forced air vent cooling?

SELECTING YOUR TRAVEL TRAILER

Must it have a good resale value, or do you expect to keep it many years — or is money no object?

Do you look forward to going on caravans to neighboring countries with other trailers?

Do you expect to use the trailer in cold weather?

Must it provide a measure of prestige?

Is it desirable that it be easily kept clean and maintained inside? Outside?

Must it have an oven? Refrigeration?

Are all utilities expected to possess the maximum in convenience of operation, utilization and ease of maintenance?

Once you have all these questions answered, at least tentatively, to your satisfaction you are ready to sally forth.

Don't be a hasty buyer. The brochures make each trailer look like the one and only, when actually there is a great deal of difference in quality between different makes. The price does not always reflect quality, either. And the original purchase price is frequently not representative of its eventual cost to the customer. Because eventually it may be resold. Also the maintenance on one may cost many times that of another.

Selecting a travel trailer is much more complicated than selecting an automobile. In the latter case they all offer much the same service, they are all good products and they all have somewhere near the same resale value for a given net cost. With the travel trailer this does not hold true. Only a few makes have good demand as used trailers and some have none at all. The quality of travel trailers is also an extreme variable. Some are sturdy and dependable. Other give nothing but trouble to the buyer.

Looking at the typical questions should give you some idea of the complexity of satisfying even your own wants, to say nothing of those of the distaff — and the children.

After you have picked many brochures and selected from them the makes that have everything you think you want, and can afford, and have read and digested the following pertinent paragraphs, you are ready to go back and have a second look at the few you are willing to consider purchasing. Take a good, long, detailed look — along with a lot of thinking — and then go home and review the packages (and prices) once more, thoroughly, before you buy.

Warranty

Almost all travel trailers are sold with a warranty — some for the life of the purchaser. But a warranty frequently means different things than the buyer infers from the verbal assurance he receives from the dealer or salesman. If you read the written warranty carefully (and interpret it in favor of the manufacturer) you may obtain a pretty good idea as to what you can expect in

SELECTING YOUR TRAVEL TRAILER

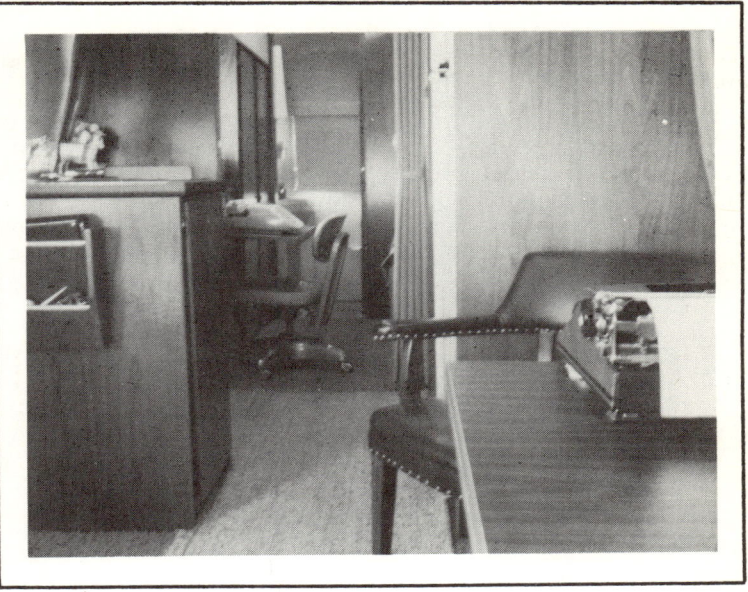

The above configuration satisfies the needs of a writing couple. Almost any combination of demands can be met — if you look around.

support of it. Again this depends upon the good faith of the manufacturer or his dealer. A few questions you might do well to ask yourself (or others) are:

Is an appointment required for warranty work at the factory and how long is the wait?

Does the trailer have to be returned to the factory, by the owner, to get warranty service? And where is the factory?

Where must the trailer be delivered for repairs to items not covered by the manufacturer's warranty and are they warranted? This category generally includes tires, wheels, axles, brake assemblies, all appliances, and other trade accessories. Appliances usually give the most trouble, although other accessories are not sacrosanct, by any means.

Does the warranty mean that a failed item will be made 'good as new'? — or merely that it will be patched up much as you would sew a patch on a torn trouser knee. The reputation of the company is your best answer to this question — and present owners afford the best source of information — ask them.

Can the dealer, and the manufacturer, be depended upon — or is either one or the other "here today and gone tomorrow"? If you risk the latter you risk both resale and warranty value.

SELECTING YOUR TRAVEL TRAILER

Extended Travel or Long Trips

If you anticipate taking long trips in your trailer you will have greater need for (a) a streamlined contour (for economy and for safe towing), (b) self-containment — water stowage under pressure, generator-supported battery supplied power, 24 hour refrigeration while parked **or** moving, sewage containment (so-called 'holding tank' or 'sanitator'), heating system, (c) comfort and convenience of stowage and furnishings, (d) dependability — tandem axle, adequate tires, sturdy construction, and (e) minimum weight to size.

Travel off Main Highways

For travel to nature parks, mountains and deserts, or to Mexico and Alaska, you will want to give greater emphasis to b, d, and e, above. For an inexpensive way to augment the battery power available to you read in Chapter 3 about a simple way to free your auto's primary battery for use in helping power your trailer facilities.

A combination rig that meets all contingencies. For fishing or hunting where you can't take the trailer, stash it and proceed on in with the camper-tow vehicle — and boat. This rig offers unlimited possibilities for the real buff.

SELECTING YOUR TRAVEL TRAILER

Winter Use

If you will be using your trailer in cold weather you want to be sure that it not only has an adequate circulatory heating system but that all water lines, and the battery, are located within the insulated envelope. Of tremendous advantage is the new Suburban Model NT-22A which, due to a special combustion system, can be left in operation while towing.

Hot Weather Use

Adequate, full-opening, windows plus two or more ceiling vents (preferably with fans) are imperative.

Caravans

Several manufacturers provide the opportunity for owners of their trailers to go on 'caravans' with other owners to other countries — principally Canada and Mexico, but occasionally to Central American countries and even to other continents. However, only the larger companies can afford to provide a satisfactory package as there is considerably more to a successful caravan than merely covering the route. Adequate arrangements must be made for parking at the various stops, for mail service, for police and highway assistance, for gasoline, water and other facilities, and for group and individual entertainment opportunities. Airstream not only handles each of these categories in an able and experienced manner (I believe that Wally Byam was years ahead of other manufacturers in this service) but they now send one or more company service trucks along with the Caravan to take care of emergency repairs to both vehicles and trailers. Caravans are now arranged and conducted by several of the leading manufacturers.

Prestige

As with most prestige items you probably pay something extra for the trailer makes that afford the greater prestige in ownership. However, this seems to work on both ends of the deal, because you also can command a higher price when you sell or trade. And don't think for a moment that you will be satisfied with this year's model two years from now. Even though my '68 offered so much more than the '65 that it seems this surely must be the 'ultimate', history assures me that two years from now (maybe even one) I will have to face the same challenge all over again.

Stowage

It is easy to go overboard here. Some makes of travel trailers are configured as if they were meant to be used as mobile homes rather than as travel trailers. Cubby holes, closets, overhead compartments and bulkheads abound everywhere. The female

SELECTING YOUR TRAVEL TRAILER

When attending group rallies, at selected recreation sites with other trailer buffs, flags are often flown. Shown here is a 'do-it-yourself' flag pole bracket, fashioned of heavy gauge aluminum and clamped to the jack shaft with hose clamps.

shopper gets very excited about all the things she can stuff in here and there — without a thought of the strain all that extra storage, when it is filled up with commodities, puts on the trailer chassis and frame and on the tow vehicle. If you purchase a travel trailer it is, presumably, with the idea of travelling. To travel economically and safely you want the minimum gear that you can live comfortably with — and you don't want all the corners stuffed with extra things you don't need. If you step into a

SELECTING YOUR TRAVEL TRAILER

trailer and immediately get a sense of openness — when you are inclined to ask yourself "Where am I going to put everything?" look closer — you may have the best trailer for the job. You are not nearly so likely to get claustrophobia — or to find yourself stalled on a grade. Good engineering in a trailer provides adequate storage, with features that make every item easy to get to, with minimal overhead shelving, and still leaves plenty of room to "live" comfortably. The overhead is no place to have a lot of weight when you are on the road, anyway.

If you are really buying a travel trailer to park it in a mobile home park for months on end, and travel only occasionally and not for very far, then you may want all the extra storage you can get — as with square corners and an 8 foot wide body. But if you intend to tow the thing then you want a stream-lined body — top, front and rear. And streamlined contours take a lot of the hazard, and most of the strain and hard work, out of towing. However, the latter characteristic will actually add one hazard — the inclination to drive faster than any vehicle with a tow should move. A heed to the warnings contained in Chapter 6 should provide some deterrent.

Weight Considerations

A final, and very important consideration is the weight of the trailer you are planning to buy. There are a number of factors involved and they have been treated at length and with care in the next chapter, Unit Harmony. The discussion on engine power and torque to weight ratio should affect your decision. In brief, you must have a tow vehicle that can handle the gross weight involved and it will be well for you to thoroughly digest all the information available on that before you buy your trailer.

Chapter 2
UNIT HARMONY

The term "unit harmony" has been selected to best represent the coordination, or compatibility, of tow vehicle, hitch and trailer. Among the considerations to be discussed in this category are the desired car size and power, trailer size and towing characteristics, hitch type, height, capacity and mounting, brake system modification and adjustment, as well as information as to how the combination should function when connected for towing. For safety reasons unit harmony deserves first consideration in any trailer towing endeavor regardless of the type trailer to be towed. Driving is, of course, important to safety but I am convinced that far more accidents with trailers occur because of a lack of unit harmony than from poor driving. Many accidents occur when mistakes in driving are made, in some cases very minor mistakes, which would not have happened had a harmonious relationship of tow vehicle and trailer existed.

Accident Causes

Among the more frequent causes of accidents are improper brake adjustment, poor axle-weight distribution, and hitch failure. Of the dozen or so trailer-involved collisions and upsets which I have either seen or investigated on the site only one would have happened had the rig been in proper harmony. The one exception resulted when the driver misjudged the time element and attempted to cross a street in front of an oncoming automobile which apparently did not have any brakes. A safe driver never puts his unit anywhere that will require another vehicle to reduce speed — for obvious reasons. He may have his attention directed elsewhere and not see you; he may have faulty brakes; or he may be a poor judge of time and distance. Be your own judge of time and distance — it's safer.

Selection of Trailer and Tow Vehicle

Let us consider the various facets of unit harmony in the order in which you will normally deal with them. First you will either purchase the trailer of your choice and then select a suitable tow car, or you already have the car with which you wish to tow and you want to select a trailer which your car is capable of towing safely. If you already have both you will want to examine the fundamental considerations given here to determine whether

UNIT HARMONY

or not your tow vehicle is adequate and if not what modifications can be incorporated in it to make it so. Or you may decide that a safe union is impossible in which event you will want to exchange one or the other.

A Mustang doing a creditable job towing a 17' Airstream 'way down in Old Mexico'. The lighter weight cars are perfectly satisfactory for towing smaller trailers.

Transmissions

If you are purchasing a vehicle for the prime purpose of towing a trailer you will want to give consideration to the type of transmission and to the rear-end ratio you choose. Here I unequivocally recommend a three-speed torque converter type automatic transmission with lock-in feature in all gears, and for those towing a heavy trailer (3500 lbs. up, factory wt.) the highest rear-end ratio available. I choose the automatic feature and the high axle ratio for the starting and acceleration torque available (this can be extremely important when you have double the normal weight to get moving) and the lock-in feature for the added safety, as well as braking economy, on down grades. A three-speed torque converter type transmission will yield at least a fifty

UNIT HARMONY

percent higher starting gear ratio (hence higher torque) than the standard 3-speed manual transmission available in either autos or pickup trucks.

Even if we consider going for a truck type tow vehicle with a heavy-duty 4-speed manual transmission, the automatic can beat it. The Chrysler torqueflyte, for example, with 1st gear ratio of 2.45 and torque converter ratio of 2.25, when coupled with the optional 3.23 rear axle ratio and the 350 h.p. engine available, yields a rear axle torque of 6,231 units as compared with 5,567 units in the Dodge truck with 4-speed manual (6.68 1st gear, 3.23 axle and 258 h.p.) and with another popular tow truck at 5,453 (7.0 1st gear, 4.1 rear axle and 190 h.p.) So far as I know there is no pick-up truck or carry-all available that provides as much power to the wheels as can be had with a passenger type auto properly equipped. An optimistic factor here is the revolution in automatic transmissions. Almost all manufacturers are changing over to the type described above. Automobiles that previously employed a beefed up torque converter alone, or a 3-speed automatic transmission alone (under various trade names) are now equipped with transmissions that incorporate both. Regardless of the make auto you decide on, I suggest that you insist on the characteristics outlined above when you select your tow car.

Stick shift buffs claim that they get more power because the manual shift allows them to keep their engine RPM higher for a given road speed, hence they have more power available. They overlook the fact that the automatic transmission we're talking about also has the manual selection capability. And although an automatic transmission is designed to shift automatically under all normal load factors, it certainly is not and cannot be designed to select, with equal accuracy, the right time to shift when burdened with twice the normal load. And this can be the case when you're climbing a steep grade with a heavy trailer. It is up to the driver to determine his best operating gear for a given speed and grade situation, and to use it.

Occasionally I read some trailer magazine columnist advising the trailerist to let the automatic transmission "do his thinking for him". Said columnist's experience must have involved only lighter weight trailers and only minor grades. Because that (recommended) practice can only result in overheating and generally poor performance if applied to a heavy tow. The higher engine speed available through use of the "manual shift" technique on your automatic transmission is, in hot weather and on steep grades, absolutely essential to keeping your tow vehicle healthy — by maintaining a cooler engine and transmission, as fluid circulation pump, water pump, and fan all maintain a faster rate of circulation. And, certainly, the transmission isn't going to shift down when descending a grade. Who would be foolish enough to descend a long steep grade (Wolf Creek Pass, U.S. 160, west of the continental divide, for instance) with a heavy tow, in 3rd

UNIT HARMONY

gear, and expect his brakes to stand up? You certainly do have to think for your transmission, going up or coming down. I find that my Chrysler transmission holds the gross load (car and trailer) of 11,600 lbs. on any highway grade (California State Route 18 at Bear Mountain, 39 at Old Baldy, for example) with only an occasional touch of the brake pedal.

When you consider the elimination of burned out clutches and gear clashing, plus the fact that you're never without engine power or engine braking while you have the clutch disengaged trying to shift into the next gear, the choice seems obvious. Add to this the fact that you have a passenger type automobile available for uses other than trailer towing when not on the road, there really doesn't seem to be any choice.

There is, however, the problem of overheating of the transmission fluid when the transmission is subjected to prolonged periods of near-maximum torque production, as on long, steep grades in hot weather. There are means of combatting this problem which will be discussed later.

Guide Lines

Manufacturers' guide lines vary. However, in general they recommend that the weight of the trailer not exceed the weight of the tow vehicle, that the largest engine available for the particular model car be selected, that the car be equipped with an automatic transmission, larger tires all around, and that a "trailer towing package" be incorporated in the new vehicle.

Let's examine these guide lines in the order listed. Presumably the idea in the first one is that if anything is going to wag it should be the tail, not the dog. Many people, in considering this guide line, become concerned about what weight is being considered — curb weight, loaded weight, or running weight (with hitch load distributed). Actually, although running weight is the weight that determines the effective balance between vehicles, it so happens that the curb weight ratio will be approximately equal to the running weight ratio — both vehicles loaded and hooked up ready to travel, with hitch weight properly distributed. So there seems little justification in spending a lot of time figuring out the latter.

However, for those of you who like to prove things out for yourselves, we will take a typical example and go through the calculations:

Let's assume that we want to mate a 3,000 pound automobile to a 3,000 pound trailer (both curb, or factory, weights). To calculate the running weight the following values are involved:

(a) Gross trailer weight will be 3,000 plus approximately a third — water in fresh water tank, hot
   water tank, gas bottles, sanitator contents, clothing, toilet gear, medicines & first aid, food, bed-

UNIT HARMONY

	ding, carpeting, beverages, books, magazines, dishes, utensils, sporting equipment, brica-brac, radio, television, linens, jewelry — all contribute to this factor	4,000 lbs.
(c)	Hitch weight will be approximately 12% of gross weight	480
(c)	Hitch weight displaced to car axles when hitched up and compensating bars in place	360
(d)	Running weight on trailer wheels (gross wt. less displaced hitch wt.)	3,640 lbs.*
(e)	Gross weight of auto will be 3,000 plus a Constant approximating 400 pounds, assuming two passengers (300 lbs., half tank of gas (70 lbs.) and tools (30 lbs.)	3,400
(f)	Running weight on car wheels (gross weight plus 75% of hitch weight (item (c)	3,760 lbs.*

The above figures, which are somewhat conservative, prove the point, that curb weight comparison is at least safe, if anything it will err on the side of caution. For example we have ignored the dead weight of the hitch (attached to the car,) weight of air conditioning package or trailer package neither of which are usually reflected in the factory weight, and additional tools and equipment which may run several hundred pounds (outboard motor, golf clubs, extra spare tire, equipment per list given in Chapter 5, etc. all of which could add up to another thousand pounds.

The guide line on engine size is, I think, a good one. A rough check on the validity of this can be had by setting up a ratio of torque units to gross load in a vehicle with which I am intimately familiar — the Chrysler Imperial with which I have towed a gross load of approximately 11,600 pounds over typical grades throughout the U.S., Canada, Alaska and Mexico, and which I consider to be satisfactory — although I have sweated out a few steep ones at less than 5 mph — the half mile grade just off U.S. Rte. 160, 8 miles north of Moab, Utah, leading to Dead Horse Point State Park (don't miss this one if you have to walk), for example, and I was almost ready to start unloading ballast, starting with my wife, the cat, and me, in that order. I intend to specify the higher 3.23 rear axle ratio on the next one.

To come up with a typical power ratio let's compute the torque units available at my rear axle and compare to the gross weight load in pounds. Multiplying torque converter ratio (2.25) by 1st gear ratio (2.45) by differential ratio (2.91) and by engine horsepower of 350 we have 5,614 units of torque. This gives a ratio of 5,614 to 11,600 or about one half unit of torque to one pound of load. I would consider this the minimum satisfactory ratio and a good way to determine if the tow vehicle you are planning to use will be adequate in a really tough haul.

Illustration showing how vehicles of approximately the same factory weight still bear the same proportionate weight when loaded and hitched up for travel.

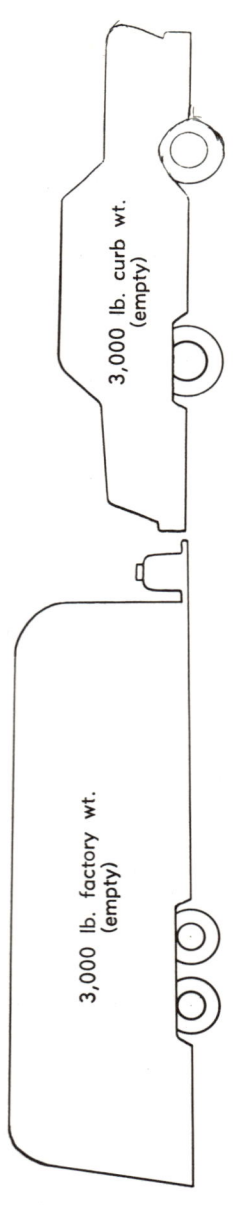

(a) Factory weights approximately equal.

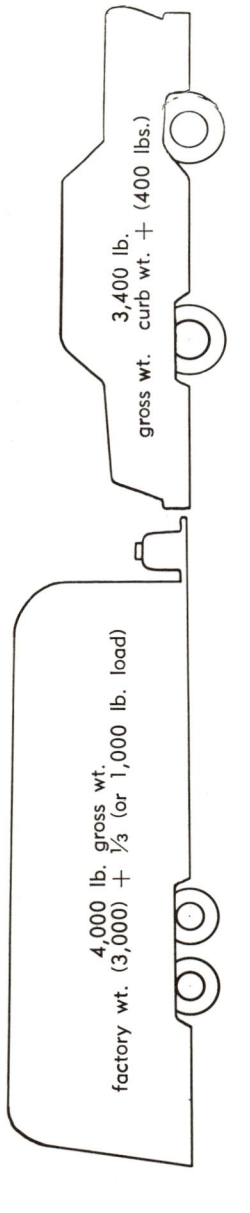

(b) **Trailer takes on more load than tow vehicle.**

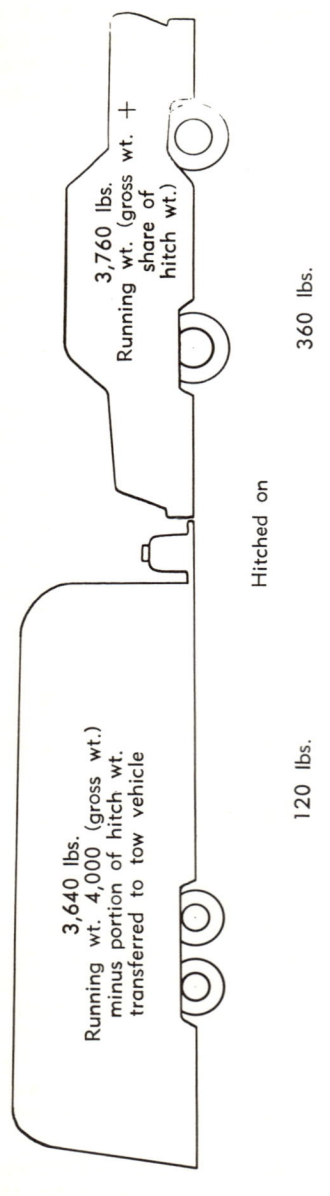

(c) **Distribution of hitch weight again equalizes weights so that loaded tow vehicle weighs as much or more than trailer.**

UNIT HARMONY

There is one ratio that I have ignored — that of ring gear diameter to outside tire diameter — but inasmuch as I can't find anything on it we will assume, for the present, that they remain pretty much the same throughout the range of automobiles available — but what happens when you go for larger tires (as recommended above and with which we concur)? If will bear, looking into in future.

The next recommendation, in favor of the automatic transmission, has, I think, been adequately supported earlier in this chapter. If not, consider the fact that Chrysler Corporation will not warrant any of their automobiles for regularly towing a heavy trailer with manual transmission. Beginning in 1957 their engineers have been on top of the trailer towing problem — and one of their first conclusions was that a manual transmission is not suitable for towing heavy trailers.

Now comes the trailer towing package. As Winston would have put it, "Nowhere can so much be had for so little." For only a few dollars, usually under fifty, the manufacturer provides heavier springs, heavier shock absorbers, a larger radiator, larger fan, heavy duty flasher and brake light switch, and sometimes the higher rear axle ratio and special trailer wiring harness. The later Chrysler makes also incorporate a larger transmission fluid cooler in the package. By all means, if you are ordering your car custom equipped, get the package.

Hitch Factors

Factors that directly affect the proper functioning of the hitch are hitch weight, rating, type, make, installation, ball height and compensating bar adjustment. Each of these factors will be discussed separately.

Hitch Weight

Safety engineers recommend that twelve to fifteen percent of the trailer gross weight (loaded) appear on the hitch. None will recommend less than ten percent, and this lesser ratio is safe only with very long trailers. As you can readily see, the tipping effect of steep inclines or accelleration becomes less as the trailer length increases, given a constant height and vertical weight distribution factor. However the planing effect produced by air currents under a trailer which is being towed with the front end too high **increases** with trailer length and must be guarded against more diligently with lower ratios of hitch weight. This latter characteristic will be discussed at greater length in a following paragraph.

Hitch weight can be largely determined by selective loading. Canned goods, books, writing materials, etc. can be stowed forforward of the axle. The water tank, if located at the front, can be kept full when travelling.

UNIT HARMONY

Too little weight not only increases the tendency to sway, or undulate, it is also likely to cause 'bucking' at the hitch, especially on slightly uneven pavement. Although stiff springing, inadequate shock absorbers, and overly-heavy compensator bars can also cause bucking.

Hitch Rating

Select a hitch which has a rating of at least 10% of your estimated gross trailer weight. In figuring gross weight add a third to the manufacturer's published factory weight (this may seem excessive but a review of the section on engine power will show the justification). For example, given a 3,000 pound trailer (curb weight at the factory) we can add 1,000 pounds to arrive at the gross weight. 12% of this is 480 lbs. which represents the absolute minimum that should be carried on a trailer of this size. Any less would be hazardous. The hitch you buy, then, must be rated at least this high, preferably a little higher as you may frequently carry more weight on the hitch than the minimum.

Hitch Type

All but the very smallest travel trailers require a compensating hitch in order to be towed safely. A compensating hitch is one which, through the use of lever-bars (called compensating bars) or other levering device, permits a part of the hitch weight to be projected, or levered, forward onto the front axle. The ratio of the horizontal distance between the hitch ball and the tow vehicle's rear axle to that between the two axles is a factor in determining if a compensating hitch is necessary, even with very light trailers. For example, my tow vehicle has approximately twice the distance between axles as between the rear axle and the hitch ball. Obviously a mere 200 pounds of hitch weight placed directly on the ball will place 300 pounds on the rear axle and, at the same time, lift 100 pounds off the front axle. Assuming that equal weight appeared on the two axles prior to hooking on to the trailer (the normal condition for family type passenger automobiles, empty) I would now have a difference of 400 pounds between front and rear axles — excessive for optimum steering action. It is obvious that a vehicle with the same axle spread and with only three feet from rear axle to hitch ball would have only 250 pounds added to the rear axle and 50 pounds of lift at the front axle for a differential axle weight of 300 pounds.

The foregoing example is merely illustrative, as we will be concerned with greater hitch weight — in the order of 400 to 900 pounds.

Hitch Make

I understand there are several compensating hitches on the market which are entirely satisfactory, among them the Bock, Robot, Equalizer, and EAZ-LIFT. I am prepared to discuss only

UNIT HARMONY

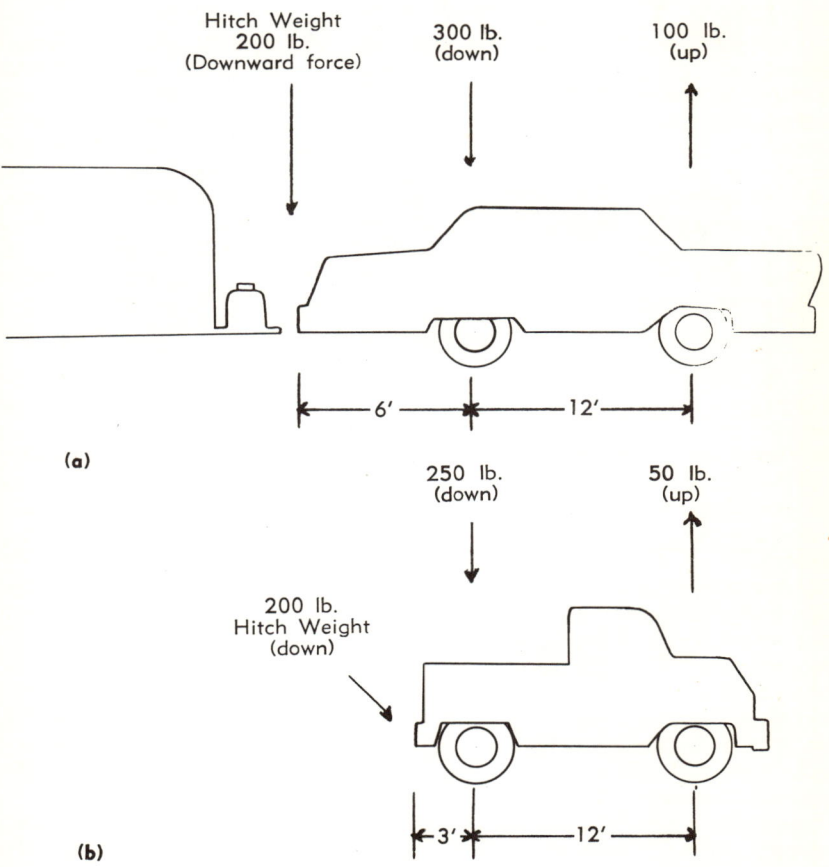

Note the comparative effects of hitch load on different types of tow vehicles. In (a), hitch weight is much more important than in (b), where weight is placed more nearly directly on the rear axle.

UNIT HARMONY

The Robot hitch. Somewhat bulkier and heavier than most, its users swear by it.

The presence of two sway-control devices in this illustration, both the Reese Magic-Cam and the Eaz-Lift, indicates the user must have learned the hard way — and possibly too well.

UNIT HARMONY

the two makes with which I am familiar, the EAZ-LIFT and the REESE. I consider both to be very good hitches, having towed with both. However, I favor the basic REESE for its compensating bar action and convenience of placement when hooking up, and the separate EAZ-LIFT Sway Control Bar (not a part of the basic hitch) over the REESE Strait-Line sway control (auxiliary to the basic hitch) because the former exerts a constant holding force which can be adjusted to suit the rig. I keep mine set at the maximum suggested range (40-lb. cam-lever torque) not only to curb self-induced and passing-vehicle induced diversion but to avert loss of control in the event of more violent maneuvers such as might result from strong wind gusts or inadvertent dropping of a wheel onto a low shoulder.

The sway control, discussed in the foregoing paragraph is, of course, the apparatus which is designed to reduce or eliminate horizontal undulation of the rig, caused by any displacement of the rear end of the tow resulting from wind draft or vacuum created by passing vehicles. I have noted an interesting characteristic in the effect on my Airstream. The taller vehicles cause no more disturbance than do the lower ones. In fact, the very tall ones, those with the bottom of the freight body five or more feet high, cause none. I've figured this must be because of the pronounced curve beginning about four feet up on the side of my trailer — there is simply no resistance to air disturbance created that high up. Even the bottom of my trailer is rounded, which probably also helps considerably to reduce the effect of low vehicles.

Hitch Installation

Have your hitch installed by a shop that has had a lot of experience with heavy hitches. Pay a preliminary visit to the shop and get the owner or foreman to explain how he goes about securing the hitch, what type of hitches he is prepared to furnish, and what the charge will be. If detailed information is not forthcoming I would immediately suspect the shop's capability and would seek help elsewhere.

Regardless of what type hitch is installed or how, all securing points should be inspected after the first few hundred miles and thereafter at intervals of two to five thousand. At the same time check all welded joints on the hitch itself. Occasionally hitches do come off and welded joints do separate. Make sure yours isn't one of them. When they do there is usually a catastophe.

In any event, be sure your hitch is one that attaches to the tow vehicle frame and not to the axle, as the axle type hitch may seriously overload the rear axle shafts, bearings, wheels and tires.

UNIT HARMONY

Hitch Ball Height

Most manufacturers specify a hitch ball height that is the proper height from ground level to the top of the ball that will provide for uniform road clearance throughout the length of the trailer. Realization of this uniform clearance is of great importance in safe towing, particularly at high speeds. If the hitch is too high the trailer will have a tendency to 'plane' — that is, the front of the trailer will try to become airborne and thus exert a lifting effect at the hitch resulting in erratic tail movement, both horizontal and vertical. There have been cases of breakaway of the tow in extreme situations. On the other hand a low hitch will establish a vacuum effect under the trailer and cause an uneconomical drag as well as a slight tendency to weave as the vacuum is disturbed or shifted by cross winds or passing vehicles. However, a slight downward tilt is to be preferred to an upward one as it will exert less deleterious influence on towing characteristics.

I find that the best results are obtained by having the hitch installed on the tow vehicle at the specified height with the vehicle loaded, just as it would be when used for towing (front seat passengers can be eliminated for this purpose as front seat weight is situated approximately midway between axles). Then front seat passenger weight, as well as the trailer hitch weight which will be placed on the rear axle (see below for explanation) will combine to bring the hitch ball down, when hooked up, a slight amount (up to 1"). This will help to avoid the occasional 'high hitch' situation when tanks are empty or weight distribution is otherwise momentarily disturbed.

Weight Compensating Bar Adjustment

Only the determination of how many links to drop in placing tension on the compensating bars remains and you will have an optimum hook-up so far as weight and alignment is concerned. The only satisfactory way to determine this, in my opinion, is on a weight basis. It can be done, perhaps well enough to get by, by measuring the relative height of the front and rear of the tow vehicle before connecting, then seeing that the same ratio is maintained with up to one inch less clearance at the rear, when compensating bars are in place. This is assuming that you have extra heavy springs at the rear, either as part of a trailer towing package or as custom replacement. (In this respect the air-filled type booster springs fail too often, for one reason or the other, to be considered by me). If you have only the original, or standard, springing the proper differential axle weight will bring the rear down considerably more than one inch.

However, a weight check after hooking up is your guarantee. Simply load both vehicles, ready for travel, and drive to a set of state highway scales (commercial scales are available in most towns and cities at concrete plants, sand and gravel pits, etc. in

UNIT HARMONY

A supreme example of how NOT to position a ball mount. The angle, or pitch, of the ball mount (or head) is reversed, making it necessary for the compensating bars to be tucked up to the last link in order to lever the proper portion of hitch weight onto the front axle. Causes tremendous twist and pull on the A-frame brackets in turning and eventually results in rupture of the brackets or supports if not corrected.

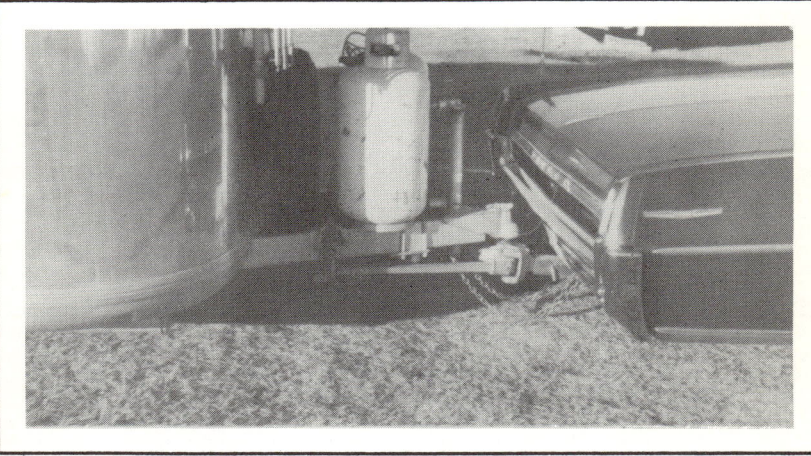

Hitch ball mounts, or heads, positioned with reverse angle, are a serious hazard and are far too common. Hitch work should never be attempted by amateurs or even by master welders — unless they know hitches, and the demands made upon them, thoroughly.

UNIT HARMONY

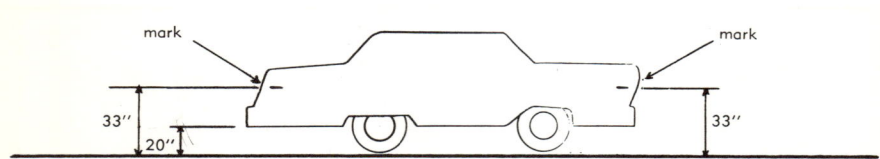

(a) Place crayon (or lipstick) mark at convenient height on front and rear of car, before hitching up.

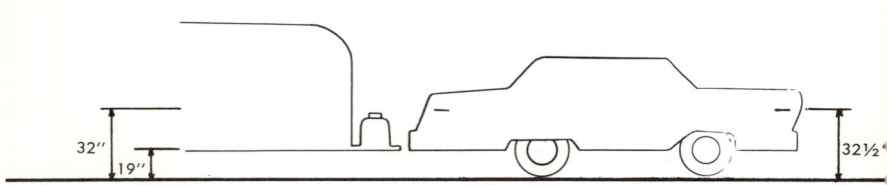

(b) Hitch up, then select the degree of compensation (using chains or means provided) necessary to achieve the optimum axle weight ratio — normally 1" differential.

Measurement method for determining amount of compensation required. If hitch ball height is specified at 20", 19" will let nose down slightly and thus avoid the undesirable "high hitch" situation of loading is shifted.

UNIT HARMONY

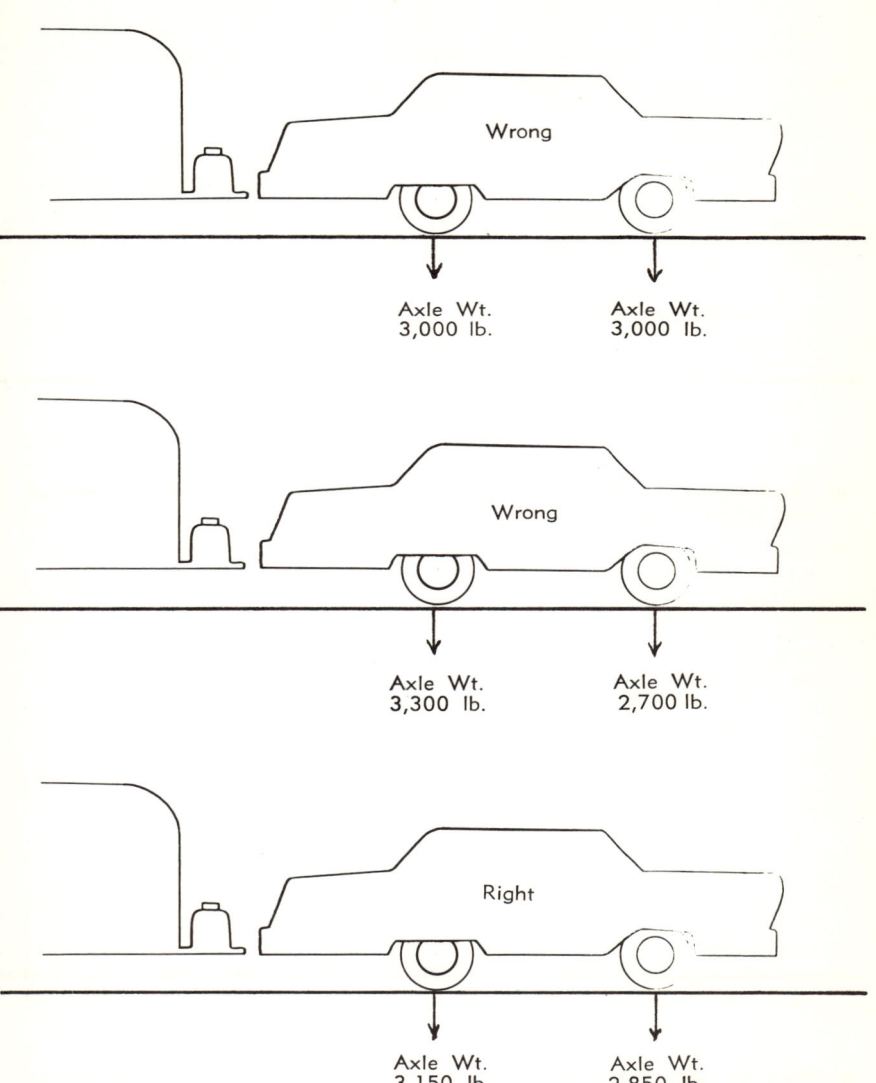

Hitch weight should be distributed so that the rear axle has two to four hundred pounds more than an equal share of gross vehicle load. Tires wear less and downhill curves are taken with less hazard.

UNIT HARMONY

the event no highway scales are handy) and obtain separate axle weights. The rear axle should now have two hundred to five hundred pounds more weight on it than there is on the front axle, depending upon the weight of your tow vehicle. The heavier the vehicle the greater differential allowed.

The goal here is to get as much more weight on the rear axle as is feasible without overloading springs, axles, and wheels and also while still leaving sufficient weight on the front axle to maintain good steering characteristics. A lightly loaded front axle is a definite hazard at higher speeds and particularly on slick pavement.

In hoisting the ends of the compensating bars to the proper chain link I find it best to employ the trailer tongue jack (for 20 to 30 turns) plus a bumper jack handle for levering the chains into place.

Turning Radius

When you are hooked on and properly compensated is a good time to check and measure the turning radius of your unit. Check it to make sure your trailer hitch has been mounted far enough to the rear to permit your tow vehicle to turn on its minimum radius without bringing the rear of the vehicle into contact with the front of your trailer. Otherwise you are sure to damage your equipment sooner or later. The measurement is for future reference in determining the capability of your unit to effect a turn in a given space. This information will come in handy more times than you can imagine. Never start a turn unless you know you can make it. Otherwise you are sure to find yourself wedged in — unable to move either way. And don't make the common mistake of assuming that you can turn in closer quarters by backing and filling — it just isn't so. The least space is required when making a hard U-turn.

Let's take the check first. Find a flat, paved area (supermarket parking lots are good, especially on a Sunday) and put your unit into a tight turn to the left (left is always good on any maneuver as you can watch the position of your tow better), holding the steering wheel just off the stop (holding hard into the stops can damage power steering components) and make a couple of complete turns. Have someone observe the start of your turn closely to be sure that no part of the tow vehicle comes in contact with any part of your trailer, that all components have sufficient clearance and that the hitch neck is riding freely on the ball. Then make a full right circle, again watching for adequate clearance, before turning left again for turning radius measurement. You will need to measure and record the diameter of your tire travel as well as the diameter of the vehicle clearance required. Your future turning spot may have unlimited clearance but marginal area suitable for wheel travel, or vice

UNIT HARMONY

versa. To establish clearance you can station two members of your family, or friends, on opposite sides of the circle, barely clear of your front bumper. To obtain your travel radius you can scatter a few handfuls of dry earth on the pavement before transcribing your circle.

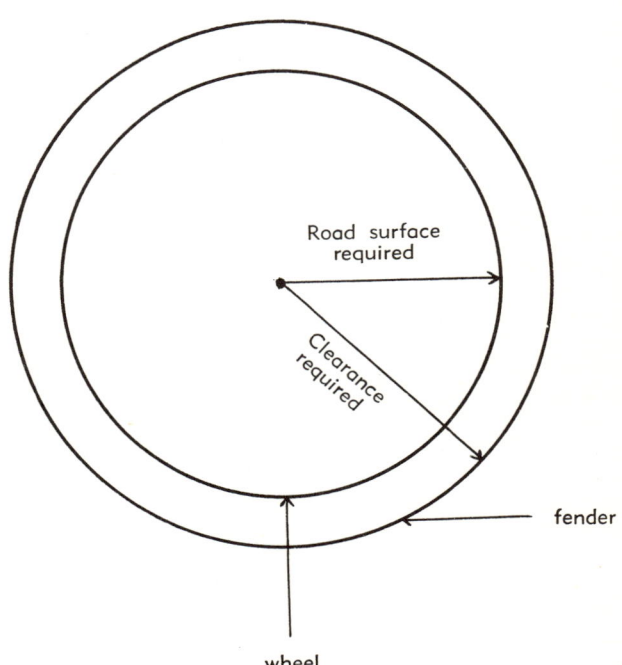

Transcribe a tight circle on dirt surface or pavement which you have dusted. Measure road surface required (inner circle), and clearance required (outer circle). Step the distance off in strides you can duplicate when the need to know arises.

UNIT HARMONY

Brake Control Circuit

An adequate brake control system will include (a) a hydraulic control operated by hydraulic pressure in unison with the tow car brakes and activated by the foot pedal or by hand, at the driver's option, and (b) a 'brake-resistor' unit which can be adjusted, by selective placement of several nichome-wire resistive elements, or by movement of a variable tap on a single element, to provide the amount of current needed at the trailer brake shoe solenoids to achieve the proper relationship between tow vehicle braking and trailer wheel braking.

Two characteristics are highly desirable in the braking system, one of which is absolutely essential. First, with emergency application of the brakes by foot pedal pressure the trailer wheels must brake approximately as strongly as those of the tow vehicle. If this relationship does not exist, hard braking in an emergency is almost sure to jack-knife the rig and cause both trailer and tow vehicle to roll over. I have personally witnessed two such episodes and attended the wake of two more, and in each case the tow car wheels were found to be doing too big a share of the braking. Second, we want smooth application of the trailer brakes (no sudden jerk), but only if this can be attained while retaining the first requirement.

Perfect alignment of the brake system (where trailer braking is exactly as effective as tow vehicle braking throughout the brake pedal stroke) is seldom realized due to the wide variation in hydraulic pressure, in brake shoe effectiveness and in tire characteristics. However, we can and must assure that the trailer will brake strongly enough to preclude jack-knifing the rig in an emergency stop. From there we do the best we can.

The only brake control system with which I am familiar (the Kelsey-Hayes) is, in my opinion, somewhat less than ideal for many automobile brake systems. Its rate of application seems to be much too high. In other words, even though the control may be set so that the car brakes engage first, the trailer brakes engage fully long before the car brakes do. The application of braking power to the vehicles should "track" better. Perhaps by the time this book is published someone will produce a device so designed. Improved operation may be available in the new Tekonsha control (which utilizes the variable tap resistance element and a somewhat different hydraulic pressure control unit.

In setting up my braking system I use the following procedure. First I set the brake control unit so that the hand lever just comes to rest against the right side of the guide channel (this channel limits brakes lever travel) when the foot pedal is fully depressed. This assures that the control unit will travel the full length of its throw for smoother application of trailer brakes. Then I arrange the nichrome-wire resistance elements of the brake-resistor unit so that trailer tires begin to slide just before

UNIT HARMONY

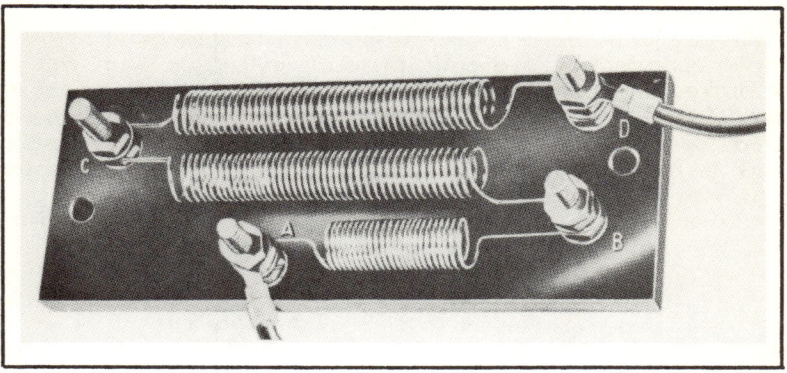

"Brake Resistor. Provides 8 variations in maximum braking current (or an infinite number if further division of the nichrome wire is effected) to suit any combination of trailer and tow vehicle weights or brake system characteristics."

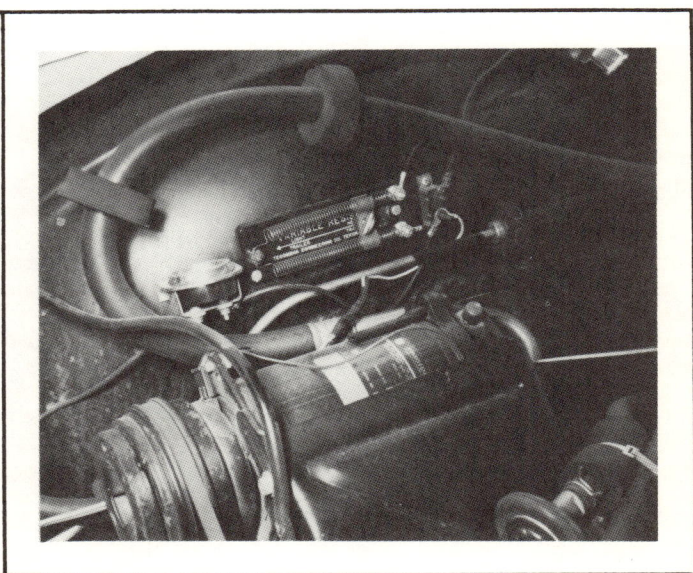

Trailer Brake Limiting Resistor — This type affords infinite variation in setting, by simply moving a thumb screw clamp, and meets an acute need for simplicity. Many trailer brakes are operated unsafely because of the difficulty of adjusting the old type.

UNIT HARMONY

"Brake Controller, actuated either by hydraulic pressure from foot pedal, or by a hand on the lever"

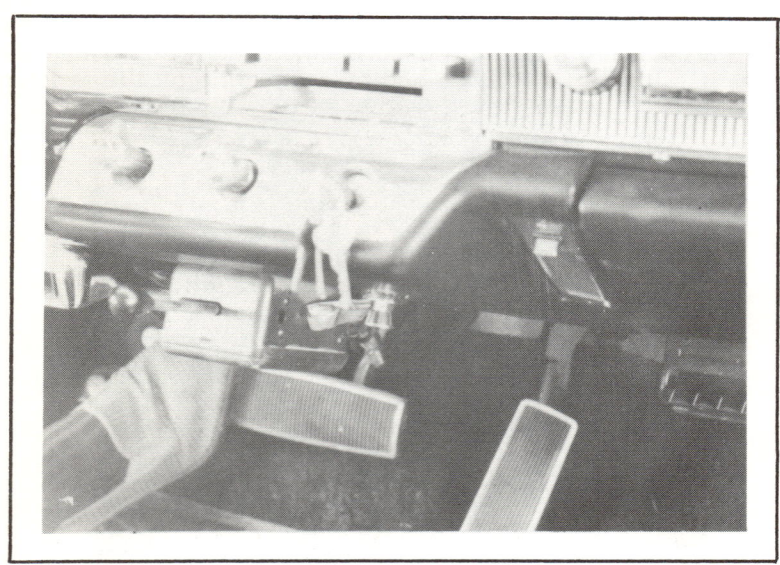

"Brake rheostat control arm in correct position (full on — but not quite touching right end of slot) with brake pedal fully depressed."

UNIT HARMONY

the tow vehicle wheels do. Braking force tests can be made on loose gravel, or on a dirt road, with less difficulty as the tires slide more readily. It might be well to remember that a greater rate of decelleration can be realized if braking force is just short of being sufficient to lock the wheels, as a sliding tire surface exerts less braking effect than one that is being "slowed" at a maximum rate (just short of locking).

In many instances the recommended arrangement of the resistor elements, as shown on the instruction sheet that accompanies the unit, will achieve the desired braking relationship. In others neither the recommended arrangement nor any of the arrangements suggested will do so. In the latter case you can create variations in the effect of the unit by halving the longer elements and thus doubling up on the paths for passing current to the brake solenoids, as discussed in the following paragraphs.

In working with this unit remember that you get the most current to the trailer brakes, hence quicker and stronger braking, with no elements in the circuit (shorted out of the picture — bypassed). However, this arrangement, which effectively eliminates the resistance-unit completely, will work only on the heaviest tows. In most cases it will result in too much trailer braking, and consequent "jerking" when brakes are applied, calling for insertion in the circuit of at least some resistance. The nearest thing to no resistance at all (if you determined that you needed some but only a very little) can be had by connecting all the resistance elements in parallel between the two brake circuit leads, or terminals. If this proves to be too much resistance, one or more of the longer elements can be stretched at the middle and doubled up — to provide even more paths for current to flow, hence less resistance and more braking. Further division of the elements can be effected if found necessary in achieving effective, yet relatively smooth, braking. There is a movable tap on the new Tekonsha element which simplifies selection of the desired resistance.

Chapter 3
OTHER SAFETY AND RELIABILITY FACTORS

Other factors affecting safety and reliability, but which are not directly associated with the harmonious relationship of tow vehicle and trailer are discussed in this chapter.

Tires

If towing a heavy trailer (gross weight over 3,500 lbs.) your automobile should be equipped with the next greater tire size above that furnished as standard equipment because of the added weight projected forward from the hitch. If you are using a truck as tow vehicle the tire size specified usually suffices.

In inflating your vehicle and trailer tires consideration must be given to safety hazard, tire hazard, tire wear and ride quality, listed and discussed in their order of importance.

Safety hazard is created when either the trailer tires on the rear tires of the tow vehicle are under inflated, especially the latter. With soft tires the tendency to sway is increased considerably, as the tire will "lean" readily with a wind gust or passing vehicle draft, as well as when moving over uneven roads. And the swaying, or "whipping" of the tow is the cause of almost every trailer upset on the highway.

Tire hazard can be the result of either too high or too low air pressure. If the pressure is too high the tire will be more easily punctured by sharp rocks, bits of steels, etc. and will be more susceptible to bruising — from rocks, bricks, and curbs. If too low the excessive degree of flexing as the wheel turns, especially at high speed, will weaken the side wall and may result in a blow-out.

Tire wear increases as the temperature of the tread rises. Under inflation results in excess flexing of the side walls with the attendant heat build-up. Over inflation will cause the center tread to wear down first, and thus shorten the usable life of the tire.

Ride quality is frequently given no attention, with the trailerist simply carrying the maximum allowed tire pressure in all tires and letting it go at that. To others, tow vehicle ride is given

SAFETY FACTORS

consideration (as a hard ride produces audible rattles and squeaks in short order, as well as nervous system reaction to more or less degree) but the trailer ride quality is ignored. Even the phenomena of caps unscrewing themselves from containers, structural seams coming unriveted, plastic structures fracturing, screws backing out of woodwork, objects climbing vertical inclines several times their height into adjacent compartments, etc. sometimes fails to arouse a suspicion that maybe the ride is harder than it should be and that over-inflated tires might be contributing to the condition. However, as the first three considerations are of more importance, the only service we can render this latter factor is to avoid inflating tires more than is necessary to achieve a reasonable degree of the three primary considerations.

My own option for tire pressures, necessarily a matter of judgment based on the above factors, plus fully loaded trailer weight (5,000 lbs. on tandem axle when hitched up), loaded car weight (3,100 lbs. front, 3,500 lbs. rear, when loaded and hitched up with its share of trailer hitch weight) is 28 lbs. front, 32 lbs. rear and 40 lbs. trailer, with consideration given to tire size and rating. These inflation pressures have worked very well through the sixty thousand plus miles of towing, as is proved by the very fine results I've had with tires, as well as an unblemished safety record.

No doubt you are wondering why the trailer should require more pressure when their share of the distributed weight is less. For two reasons, actually. First, any one tire on a tandem axle assembly frequently has to support considerably more than its static distribution of the load as, for instance, when on a steep side slope with the paired tire in a depression. In such a situation one tire may momentarily support up to one-half the dynamic trailer weight. On an uneven road surface each tire may be supporting more than its static share of the load as much as half the time. This characteristic furnishes the primary justification for the use of 6-ply tires — which is the second reason for the higher inflation pressure on the trailer. Six-ply tires develop heat much faster, with the same degree of flexing, than do 4-ply tires, hence they should stand a little taller.

A rule of thumb suggested by some tire industry representatives is that a good tire can safely carry up to ten pounds per ply (i.e. 40 lbs. for a 4-ply tire, 60 lbs. for a 6-ply). We are well within that restriction in this case.

Another rule of thumb frequently offered is that any tire which builds up to more than 120% of its cold pressure when hot is underinflated. For example, a tire inflated to 30 lbs. when cold should not build up to more than 36 lbs. If it does so, more air should be added. For an illustration, I tried operating my trailer tires (6-ply tubeless) at 35 lbs. for the softer ride, but they consistently built up to 50 lbs. pressure even though they appeared to stand fully elevated. When inflated to 40 lbs. cold they remained under 50 lbs. when hot.

SAFETY FACTORS

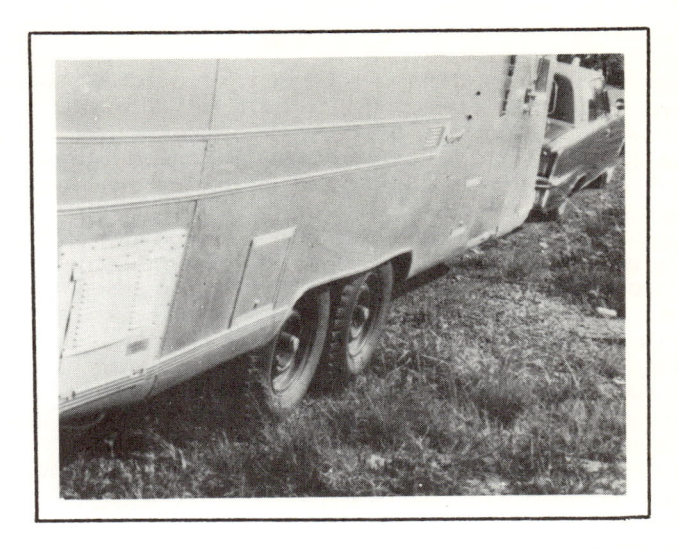

"The above situation sometimes results, with one trailer tire bearing most of the trailer weight momentarily (trailer on hillside and one of the burdened tires in a depression)."

"Dura-torque axle enables removal of wheel and tire for travelling on to service point — by simply pulling paired wheel up on 4" block."

SAFETY FACTORS

Spare Tire

The question concerning the need for a trailer spare tire is frequently debated among trailer buffs. This is pretty much a matter of individual preference, but I think a spare would be mandatory for a single axle trailer. The need for a spare for tandem axle trailers is, I think, a matter of axle make. If you have a tandem axle that will permit you to remove one wheel and tire while you proceed on down the highway to the nearest service station, as with Airstream's Dura-Torque, then the added weight of a wheel and tire simply is not justified. I carried a trailer spare mounted on the front of my '65 Airstream (cursing the extra 120 pounds on the hitch every time I had to jack it up) for a year — and 30,000 miles — during which time I suffered seven flats (all nail punctures) and each time it was simpler to remove the wheel and proceed to the nearest service station than to mount the spare. And the paired tire was none the worse for it. I gave the wheel and tire to a needy trailerist in the high desert and threw the mount away — haven't missed it since, either.

Mirrors

Choose your mirrors carefully. After trying out the fender mounting type, the window-inset type, and the door edge type I go for the fender mirror all the way. This position allows for a constant awareness, thru peripheral vision, of traffic approaching on both sides. However, they should be mounted as near the driver as windshield configuration and wiper blade pattern will permit — you do have to drive in the rain some times. Of course, the fender mount, being further away from the eye of the viewer, provides a narrower field of vision. But no rear-view mirror will show a vehicle which is already in passing position, hence the driver must glance back and to the side anyway — so a few extra degrees here won't matter.

You can save yourself some grief if you reduce the extension on your mirrors to the minimum that you need. No amount of extension will let you see the motor bike or the small sports car directly behind you. So inasmuch as you can't do anything about that area — forget it. Adjust (or modify) your mirror legs so that the center of the mirror is in line with the outside skin of your trailer. Then, when the mirror is deflected so that you can just see the side of your trailer in the extreme near side of the mirror, you will have the most advantageous set-up available to you. The reason for minimum extension should be obvious — that much less liklihood of you getting them knocked off. An auto dealer out west told me he sells more mirrors singly than in pairs, and that he frequently hears the harrowing details. I've had my share — on a narrow street in a small town in Maryland my right side mirror entered the lists for a joust with a West-Coast type truck mirror — and lost the decision. In Oregon I

SAFETY FACTORS

"Mirror rigged way out like this is invitation to disaster."

"Properly mounted mirrors provide for accurate backing (simply keep the trailer side in line) and greatly decrease the liklihood of having them stripped off by passing vehicles"

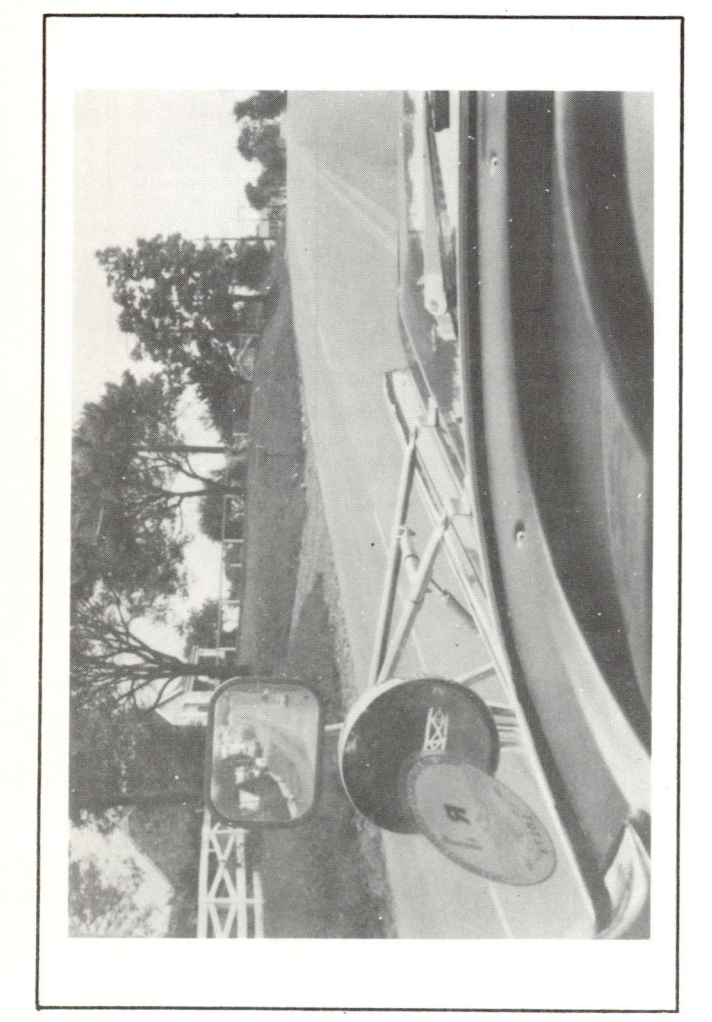

"A view to the fore shows how fender mirrors keep you aware of what is developing behind you, thru peripheral vision — without having to take your eyes from the road. Keeps you aware of the width of your own rig, also.

SAFETY FACTORS

Improperly positioned mirrors can add serious hazard. In the illustration above the mirrors are on the driver's eye level, effectively blocking his view of a considerable segment. This prevalent fault is found in many fender mirror installations.

Most fender mirrors can be positioned BELOW the pivot, as shown here, to avoid obstructing the critical viewing area. The pivoting arm may have to be altered in shape to permit the mirror to be drawn in out of the way of passing vehicles when positioned in this manner.

SAFETY FACTORS

lost one mirror to a "crabbing" truck while parked at the curb, and the second one (the trucking firm bought me a new one) one hour later to a man in a hurry on a narrow bridge. His outside mirror and mine collided.

Ease of placement and removal should not be overlooked. If either is somewhat of a task the tendency is to avoid removal — and thereby trouble is frequently encountered. A trailer in tow is easily spotted, and avoided; extension mirrors not nearly so much so. Besides causing accidents their presence sometimes earns traffic tickets.

Another advantage of the fender mount is that you are continually aware of your rig's extra width and are much less likely to maneuver too closely to buildings, abuttments, poles, etc.

Fans

Some automobiles equipped with air conditioning utilize a "variable speed" high capacity fan which has a top RPM of about 1700. By use of a silicone clutch the fan blade is decoupled from the crank shaft beyond that speed (representing a road speed of about thirty-nine MPH in high gear) to the extent that no increase above 1700 is realized. This provides for adequate cooling at idling and lower speeds and makes for much quieter operation at higher speeds than would otherwise be possible. With no tow the car's ground speed is sufficient to maintain adequate air cooling at the higher speeds even with the fan held at the lower RPM. However, towing a heavy trailer on a steep grade you frequently need to use second and first gears. You can readily see that in many situations, with the motor turning four or five thousand RPM and the road speed five to fifteen MPH, a fan speed of 1700 RPM is not sufficient to keep the motor from overheating. The solution is to install a direct-drive fan with the same or greater capacity than the original. If your dealer cannot provide this modification, try the large air-conditioning facility (one that installs air conditioners in automobiles on a custom basis, after delivery).

However, most late model autos with factory installed air conditioning employ a temperature actuated fan clutch which engages as the temperature of the engine rises. If your engine overheats, and you have this type fan, have it checked. Therein may lie your trouble.

Gauges

Some cars are equipped with warning (popularly called "idiot") lights in lieu of gauges. Towing a trailer you need more current information than is available from these signals. On a steep grade in hot weather you can damage your engine very easily. What are you going to do if you are on a steep grade a mile or so from a turnout and your engine temperature suddenly

SAFETY FACTORS

shows red? The only acceptable solution is to have a gauge installed so that you at all times are aware of your engine temperature. Lack of awareness of your charging rate can be inconvenient, also, if not disastrous.

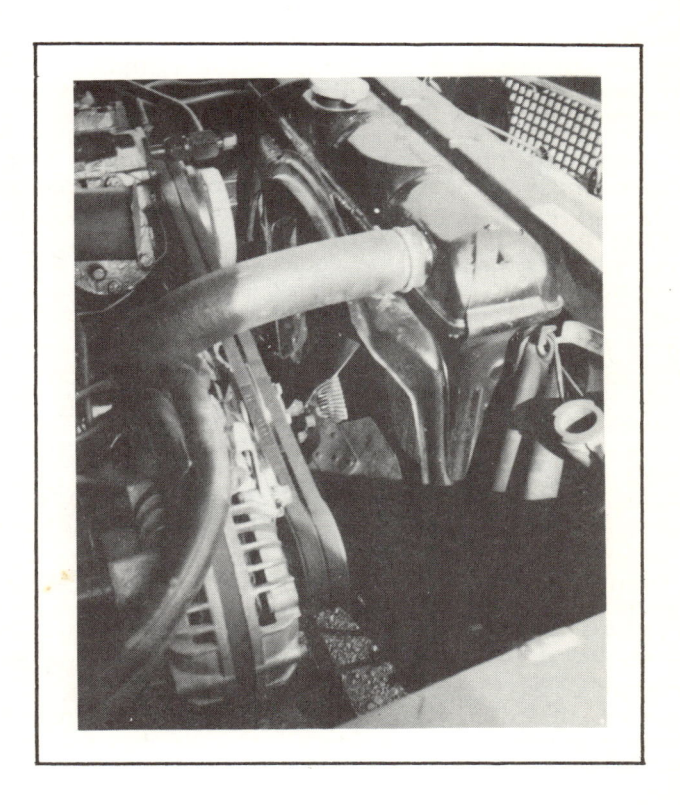

"Fluid drive fan, with silicone clutch that lets fan 'decouple' at speeds above 1700 RPM. Conversely, direct drive coupling shown at right enables fan to turn at higher speeds with engine, thereby keeping the coolant (hence engine and transmission) cool in heavy pulls at high engine RPM."

SAFETY FACTORS

Transmission Fluid Cooler

The Hayden transmission cooler (available at trailer supply stores), which is an air fin type, has good support from the travel trailer industry, from its users, and from some auto manufacturers. However, the latter do not make it a requirement so far as their warranty is affected which would indicate that, to a considerable extent, they consider it a "window dressing". And their trailer towing package does include a larger radiator with accompanying increase in transmission fluid cooling capability. The conclusion to be drawn, then, is that if you have an adequately powered tow vehicle (refer to the discussion of engine size and power ratio, Chapter 1) and the trailer towing package you should not require an auxiliary cooler.

You will want to keep a close watch on both engine oil and transmission fluid, anyway, for signs of overheating. Engine oil will darken and become dirty; transmission oil will darken and begin to smell burnt. If such indications are detected in the fluid you can then have the cooler installed.

In view of the cost of the cooler (about eighty dollars, installed — and an authorized dealer overhaul will probably cost less) perhaps you would like first to examine your driving technique before making a decision.

However, if you do have one installed I recommend it be connected in series with your auto's present cooler (definitely on the output side of it) and not, as the instructions call for, in place of it. Granted that the radiator's capability to cool the engine is somewhat enhanced by elimination of transmission fluid cooling, the incremental improvement in engine cooling which results does not justify the risk to the transmission with only the auxiliary fluid cooler in the system.

I personally suffered a transmission failure from overheating with only the auxiliary cooler connected and I have heard of several others. Since resorting to both cooling methods (by connecting in series) I have travelled the same routes, plus even more arduous ones, with no further difficulty.

Transfer Differentials

Most auto manufacturers now have special differentials available that shift driving power to the wheel that has the traction (called Posi-Traction, Sure-Grip, etc.) at a cost of about $40.00. This feature is certainly worth that to the trailerist, if just to give him the assurance he needs to allow him to park in out-of-the-way places and off the road when he needs to stop and yet the outside of the highway shoulder looks doubtful. Then, of course, there is the unforseen instance when the ground was softer than it looked, or a rain came up while parked overnight or otherwise firm surface.

Chapter 4
LEVELLING AND HOOKING UP

After taking possession of your trailer you will probably want to obtain accommodations at a mobile-home park for a day or two while you equip your trailer with necessary household effects, clothing and groceries. This is also a good time to check out all the utilities (assuming your trailer has them) so that any malfunction can be corrected while you are still near at home and perhaps near the dealer or individual from whom you bought your trailer.

Levelling

When you have selected your site and driven in (trailer parking technique is covered in the chapter on driving) you will want to level your trailer, from right to left, before unhooking. Aside from the comfort angle, some refrigerators will not work properly unless level, or nearly so. Even a slight tilt will degrade the performance of some, although I find my Dometic can accommodate a few degrees tilt to the rear of the box very well. I understand that the evaporator plate, upon which the refrigerant drops and flows, has to be substantially level so that the refrigerant has time to evaporate before it runs off the plate and starts to recirculate through the condenser — hence the poor functioning, if not level. They work okay when the trailer is moving as the evaporator plate is always shifting its plane.

You can probably bum around each time you park and find enough old boards or blocks to get your trailer level, but in my opinion the space and weight taken up by runner blocks are justified by the convenience they afford. I use two pieces of 2" x 6" redwood 8" in length and two pieces of 4" x 6" redwood 16" long, the latter with half their length cut on an incline to permit the trailer to be pulled up on them. Combinations of these four blocks have enabled me to achieve a level situation in all but very few situations. They also afford sufficient flexibility to facilitate leveling the wheels when parking for several days with the trailer nose down, or up, and there might be some warping of the dura-torque axle if the paired wheels were not substantially level with the trailer frame.

47

"Combination of 2" blocks and 4" inclined blocks permit expeditious leveling. Here is shown a maximum lift on one side of nearly six inches. If you are on a slope greater than this you shouldn't park there, anyway."

Using a 16 or 20 ounce rubber hammer, drive all four chocks in snugly to insure that trailer nose does not swing downhill. Remember that tires shrink when they are cool, which is why many custom aluminum blocks are not satisfactory — they can't be driven in as snugly as wood."

LEVELLING AND HOOKING UP

Chocks

I keep on hand four 7½" blocks cut from a 4 x 4 and then cut thru opposite corners. This angle provides the best slope for wedging between tire and ground. When wedging I drive the block under the tire with a 16 oz. rubber hammer (the hammer is also useful in securing hub-cabs). When I need to chock a wheel that is resting on the slope of the runner block I use two chocks, driving them in simultaneously, one under the other.

Dolly Wheel and Jack Pad

It is a good idea to use your jack pad and dolly wheel any time you unhitch your tow vehicle. The jack pad helps keep your trailer from moving around (it fits the dolly wheel closely) and the presence of the nose wheel reduces the amount you have to extend the jack shaft and is also good insurance against having your jack shaft slip off and bury itself. The dolly wheel can then be used to advantage in backing the front end of the trailer around as sometimes becomes necessary when you have ventured into soft ground or into close quarters where you can't pull out without changing directions.

Unhitching

Before unhitching disconnect the electric lead, the safety chains and the emergency break-away line. Release the auxiliary sway-control bar, if you have one. To unhitch, jack the nose up high enough so that the compensator bars can be dropped easily then remove and stow the bars. With the EAZ-LIFT a good trick on stowing the bars is to reinsert them in the hitch head after it has been removed from the tow vehicle and latched back into the nose.
Theft of hitch head and bars can readily be discouraged by padlocking the bars together (thru the chain links) and padlocking the hitch safety catch. The bars have to be swung forward for disengaging from the head, and locking them together prevents this movement.

Stabilizing

If you are going to stabilize the trailer now is the time to do it — before you connect the utilities. The simplest and most effortless way to do this is to lower the tongue jack twenty to thirty turns (depending upon how stable you want your trailer), place the stabilizer jacks snugly under the rear at the proper locations, and jack the nose back up until level. If you are using front stabilizers simply crank on a few more turns, place the front stabilizers and let the tongue back down level again.
A note of caution — be sure you know where the stabilizer jacks should be placed. On longer Airstream models there are

LEVELLING AND HOOKING UP

"Dolly wheel can't roll or slip out of pad, pad won't slip, and height of wheel reduces amount of cranking required to lower and raise the jack."

"Nose cranked up twenty or thirty turns to remove tension from compensator bar chains."

"Hitch head (or ball-mount) and bars can be stowed securely, or locked, as shown above. Bearing points are thus protected from the weather."

LEVELLING AND HOOKING UP

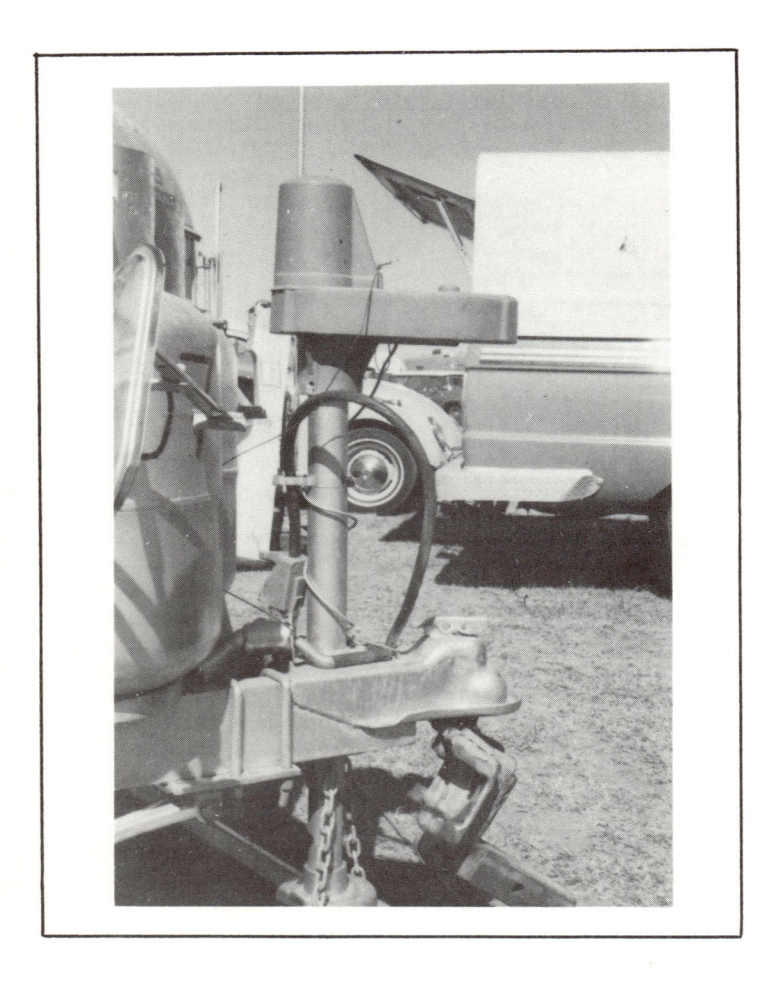

Side view of the electric jacking motor used in lieu of the hand crank. Note also the spring-clamp, secured to the shaft, for stowing the 7-way electrical connector.

LEVELLING AND HOOKING UP

small aluminum patches a short distance behind each rear wheel marking the correct spot. Although Airstream's latest instruction is only to the effect that these support points should be used if a considerable amount of the trailer weight is involved (to avoid buckling the skin at the top, I believe), I prefer to use them because if supported at the extreme rear there is sufficient flexibility in my trailer body to put a slight bow in the floor — in the '65, which had the bathtub drain at the rear of the tub, supporting at the rear trapped water in the tub so that it had to be sponged out each time. The support points provide a level trailer floor. Further, there is always the possibility that I might forget (again) and jack the front all the way up without removing the rear stabilizers — and that is just what we're cautioned about — too much weight supported front and rear.

Water Hose Connection

If your fresh water hose connects to the piping system inside the trailer be absolutely certain that the connection is water tight and that it cannot be dislodged by someone moving your water hose around outside the trailer. The number of water soaked floors and carpeting, resulting from insufficient attention to this detail, is legend. After suffering a soaked carpet I chose to move the hose connection outside the trailer by soldering a short length of half inch copper tubing into position and conducting it through a hole (drilled thru both plywood and aluminum sheath with a ¾" flat hi-speed wood drill) in the bottom of the trailer. The same fitting that connects to the hose inside works just as well outside. However, if you make this modification be sure your connection projects out into the weather as short a distance as practicable and yet sufficient to enable a firm hand grip when connecting and disconnecting the water hose.

Airstream solved this problem in the '67 models by locating a recessed drain area directly under the connection, which leads any leaked water below the floor and hence thru the belly pan to the ground. Although the location of the hose coupling is too confined to allow a good hand hold for tightening, two pairs of common pliers can be used successfully. An inside connection is certainly to be preferred — it eliminates an unsightly pipe fitting projecting outside the trailer and it reduces the chances of theft. In purchasing your water hose for a '67 Airstream remember to confine your selection to ½" thin-wall or 7/16" thick-wall hose. Otherwise you can't lead it through the 'drop-door' opening provided in the rear access panel. In the 68's it has already been led outside.

Lighting Appliances

When lighting the pilots remember that it sometimes takes several seconds for sufficient gas to get to the pilot orifice to

LEVELLING AND HOOKING UP

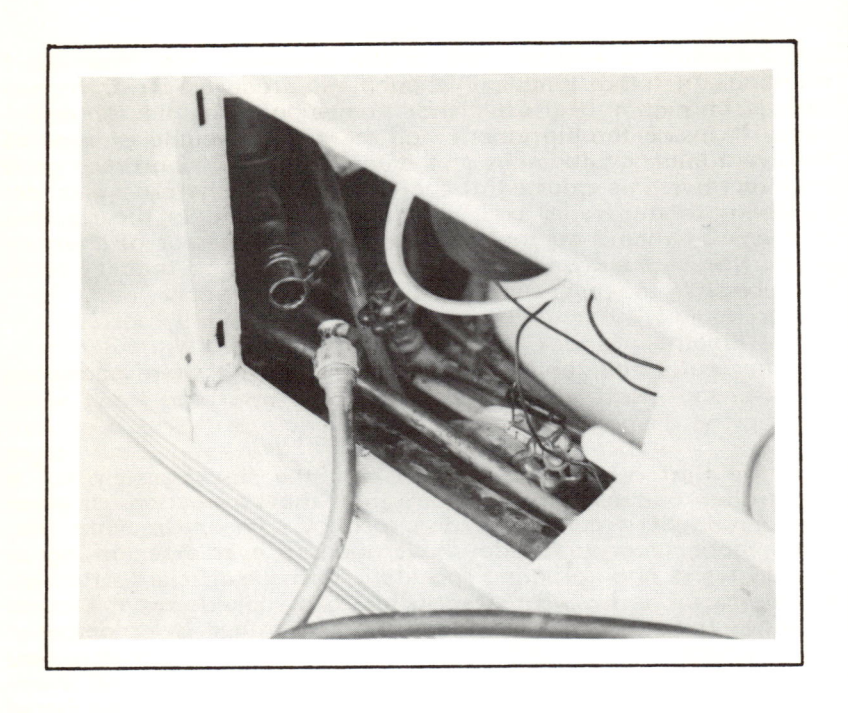

"To save skinned knuckles and short temper, employ a quick-disconnect, "Quick-Tite" for your inside water hose connection."

ignite. This is especially true of appliances furtherest from the gas bottles. I've found several lawyer and doctor types making a ritual of removing the pilot adjustment cover and opening the pilot wider because, as they said, "it wouldn't light without it", when a few seconds wait, with the pilot valve depressed, would have saved all that trouble.

I haven't yet found a pilot that couldn't be lighted with a household match, except in a high wind, but the battery-ignited liquid gas type of lighter makes it considerably easier. It ignites the flame after you get it right where you want it and saves you bruised elbows and knees in some cases. However, since I couldn't get the first one I bought to work after the first week or two — and upon attempting to borrow one from two neighbors found theirs weren't in working order either — I use a match. In sixty knot winds in the high desert I sometimes found it necessary to break out my Bernz-O-Matic torch in order to get a flame through the access door without the draft blowing it

LEVELLING AND HOOKING UP

out, even with a window open on the windward side. However, I think I've got that problem licked now. I use an old-fashioned household match (the kind that comes in large boxes) and I strike it inside the furnace. I had to move a couple of runs of flexible tubing a few inches, in order to get my hand into good position, but I'm no longer dependent upon anything less dependable than a household match. Actually, I don't have this problem anymore. My '68 Airstream has a new type furnace which stays lighted under all conditions, and whose pilot is readily accessible if you do have to light it.

Refrigerator

My refrigerator (a Dometic) lights from the front by means of a flint on the end of a rod which you rotate by hand while holding the gas valve open, or from the outside access door with a match — in case the flint doesn't work. However, don't forget that the flint can be adjusted to continue functioning after it wears down and quits. If your refrigerator won't stay lighted when you are on the road try placing a 12" x 12" rubber floor tile, foam rubber rug backing, or welcome mat over the opening in the floor and closing up the crack under the inside access panel. Of course, in warm weather, you will have to remove the cover when you're parked or your refrigerator will not work properly.

You may want to drill a 1/8" hole in the front panel so you can check the flame easily. It beats removing the panel every time you are in doubt. The '68 Airstream now has the panel hinged at the bottom for quick inspection, obviating the need for a peep hole.

Connecting Sewer Hose

In addition to the length of strong cord which I keep tied to the business end of the sewer hose for lashing it in place at the sewer inlet, I also keep a plastic elbow clamped to the business end to facilitate fitting to the sewer.

On the input end of the sewer hose (that connects to the trailer outlet) I found it advisable to secure the dog-eared plastic connector, that latches into the trailer sewer line terminal, to the sewer hose with both Epoxy glue and a hose clamp — because of the obvious hazard when twisting the connector into position. An inadvertently loosened connector here can cause even more trouble than one at the other end of the hose.

Auxiliary Drain Hose for Wash Water

As you will frequently stop for lunch or for overnight where you will not want to hook up (or where hook-ups are not available) and you will not want your wash water to drain on the pavement, or in an area where it will be offensive to other users of your parking facility, you will want to provide yourself with

LEVELLING AND HOOKING UP

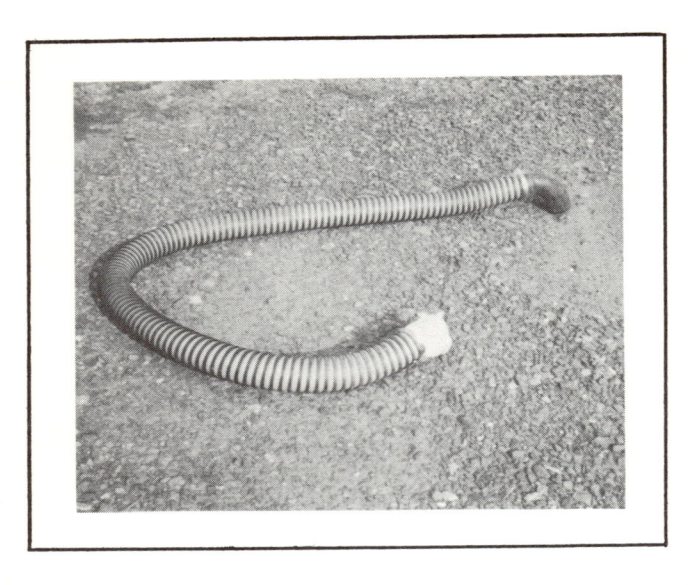

"It is advisable to secure the plastic type connector (Sanitator end) of the sewer hose with Epoxy glue as well as a clamp. An elbow on the business end of the hose simplifies fitting into the sewer inlet."

the new waste drain cap which is cast with an integral hose fitting. It takes only a few seconds to connect a 20 or 25 ft. length of ⅝ flexible hose to it and carry the end of the hose to a grassy or leafy area, or into a drain or nearby pocket of sand where the water will dissipate without making an unsightly mark. Good practice otherwise demands that the trailerist catch his drainage water in a bucket and carry it to a similar suitable dumping area anytime he is parked near others, on pavement, in public parks, or anywhere else where drainage might be offensive to others. If you are given permission to park overnight in a service station or in a supermarket lot, for instance, the manager will appreciate your attention to this detail — and the drain hose makes everything clean, quick and simple.

Water Hose Selection

While we're on the subject of hoses I would like to recommend that you choose your water hose with care. Get a good quality hose that will not impart a foreign flavor to the water that passes through it (even when lying in the hot sun) and which will remain flexible in cold weather. I carry a short length (15') of 7/16" hose for hook-ups and 50 ft. of ⅝" for auxiliary use (car washing, trailer washing, etc.) Then I insert a "Y" fitting

"Utilizing the new plastic cap with hose drain, together with a 25-ft. length of hose, enables you to drain your wash water into some suitable area — grass patch, sand wash, undergrowth, etc."

LEVELLING AND HOOKING UP

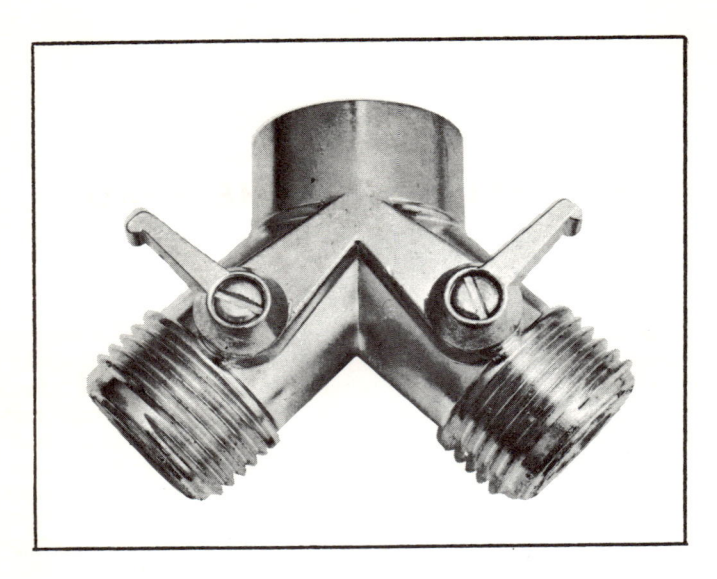

"A shut-off type water "Y", handy for auxiliary use of water supply, or for a buddy."

cut-off valve type, available at Wally Bram stores) at the water tap so that I can connect the auxiliary hose anytime I want to use it. This "Y" also serves for any other trailer that may come by and want to share my water source.

Chapter 5
PREPARING FOR THE ROAD

At the end of this chapter is a check-off list. After towing my Airstream 90,000 miles, over almost every imaginable kind of terrain and in all sorts of weather, I still use the check-off list to insure that I am truly "ready for the road" and not just 'almost' ready. It is so easy to do everything but one, and thus to pay dearly for the one omission. I have known trailerists who ignore the check-off list as something beneath their degree of competence to have suffered the following consequences: a) dragged the dolly wheel several blocks, with the hitch weight on it, mauling it beyond recognition, b) deposited part of the television antenna in a tree, c) shorted a power line with the radio whip antenna, d) lost a liquid gas bottle while travelling 60 MPH on the Pennsylvania turnpike, e) flushed the toilet onto a public street under the impression that the holding tank cut-off valve was of course closed, f) dragged open side windows off against various obstacles, g) wrapped an entry door around a lamp post, h) suffered numerous caved in trailer sides from said entry door swinging open (being in an unlocked state, i) left calling cards on numerous other vehicles and street curbs by means of a lowered doorstep, j) suffered failure of the water pump from hours of continuous running (switch left on while travelling), k) suffered broken heirlooms, dishes, food containers, etc., l) lost all refrigerator contents onto floor (what a mess) occasionally to permanently stain the carpeting, m) collided with other vehicles when tow vehicle brakes (helped not at all by the dangling 7-way plug at the front of the trailer) failed to stop in the anticipated distance, n) left behind many items of road gear (blocks, jacks, stabilizers, door mats, compartment cover doors, pets, children, and many, many more casualties that need not have been incurred — had a check-off list been employed.

Maybe the type that had rather experience the above misfortunes than use a check-off list are some of Dr. Berne's patients suffering from a persecution complex, the "Why do these things always happen to me?" type. Personally I can better afford the check-off list.

Inasmuch as the performance of some of the chores may not "come naturally" I will use this space to elaborate somewhat on a few of them.

PREPARING FOR THE ROAD

Safety Brake Cable — Item 5 (refer to check-off list): The wire safety cable which is designed to automatically complete an electric circuit between trailer battery and electric trailer brakes, thereby locking them, anytime the trailer breaks loose from the tow vehicle, should be secured to the car body or bumper and not to any part of the hitch. A high percentage of separations are the result of hitch failure. As you can readily see, a safety cable which is attached to any part of the hitch which stays with the trailer, upon separation, is not going to function. Or if it does, the emergency braking may come late. I've seen one example of each. The separation where the cable was attached to the car bumper left the trailer sitting in the middle of the highway (Alaska Hwy. 1) undamaged. The other one resulted in a complete loss — a brand new trailer rolled off Interstate 95 north of Richmond, all the way to the bottom of a 100 foot slope. The safety cable was still secured firmly behind the safety pin that locks the hitch head bolt in place — and the entire hitch, somewhat mauled, was still very much attached to the trailer tongue. The unit, passing a huge van at high speed, and with no sway control, had gone into oscillation to sufficient degree to rip the hitch loose from the frame (examination showed that it had not been properly secured). Had the safety cable been secured to the tow vehicle the trailer might very well have remained on the pavement — contents rearranged a bit no doubt — but upright and relatively unharmed. The proper functioning of the emergency braking circuit is of even greater importance on two-way highways where the trailer might be free to continue rolling into the opposite lane and into oncoming traffic.

7-Way Connector — Item 6: All cable functions except the charge line can be readily checked before you start out. Lights can be checked visually and trailer brakes can be heard engaging when the brake pedal is depressed. You can normally be sure of charging circuit completion only if you have an ammeter installed in series with the charge line, which is a good idea anyway as that way you can know how effectively your trailer battery is being charged. (If you are disappointed at what you see, refer to the section on batteries in Chapter 3.)

Rock-shield — Item 3: A rock-shield for the front window is likely to save you considerable trouble. The incidence of rocks and gravel striking windshields is quite high, usually the rocks are picked up by construction trucks on the job and thrown loose after they get onto the pavement and up to cruising speed. On gravel roads they are a constant threat, even to shatter-proof windshields — and to window glass they are calamitous. If you have the new Corning chemically tempered window glass the risk is much less, of course, but Airstream, although they now use the Corning product exclusively, provides a rock-shield as standard equipment for the front window.

"Safety brake cable — the little gem that will stop your trailer, by locking all trailer wheels electrically, if your tow vehicle should, for any reason, become separated from your trailer."

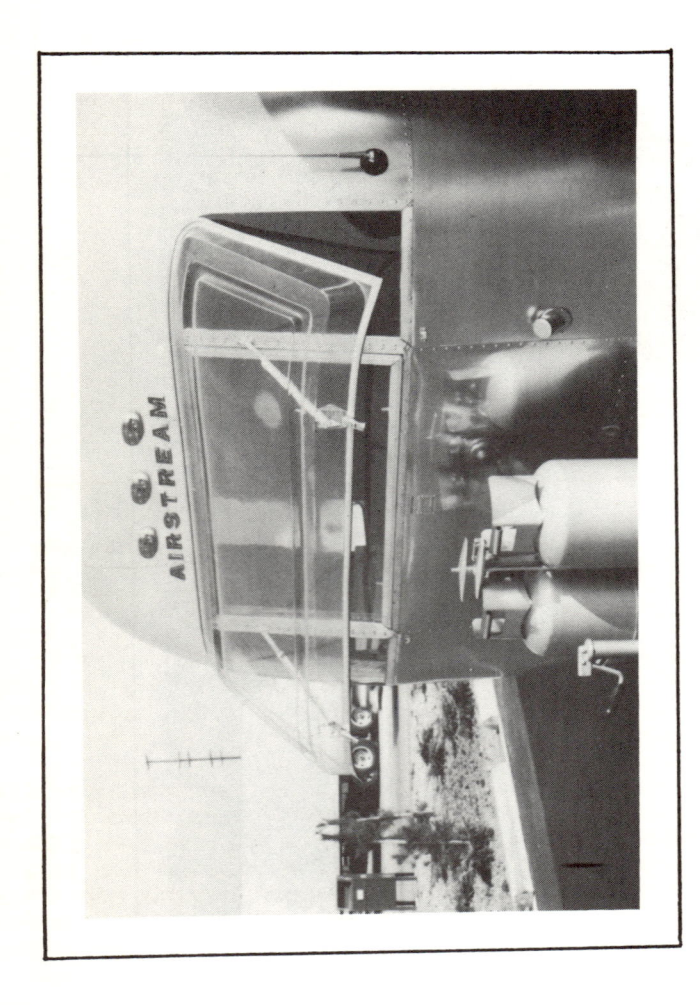

"Rock shield, which doubles as a window awning, is a must if you intend to do any considerable amount of travelling."

PREPARING FOR THE ROAD

"Sewer hose can be cleaned thoroughly by injecting a liberal quantity of detergent into a trap, formed by draping the hose over a block, and squirting water until the hose is full. Rinse once, and you've a clean hose. Hose shown is all-weather type."

Windows — Item 9: Windows can be checked from outside, in seconds, to determine if they are secured. Simply walk around the trailer, tapping each lower corner with the fat side of your fist — if they don't bounce they're latched.

Sewage Hose — Item 13: I use a pistol grip hose nozzle to clean the sewer hose. Leave it connected into the sewer and remove the other end from the trailer. Drape the hose over a block so that it forms a deep trap and fill the trap with the nozzle, first squirting a liberal quantity of detergent into the trap. Once the trap if full raise the end of the hose quickly to force a full stream of soapy water thru the length of the hose. One or two rinses similarly executed and the hose is clean and odor free.

Gas Bottles — Item 7: Make a habit of securing your gas bottles (turning the clamp that secures them down tightly) as soon as you have the gas line connected and before you open the gas valve. If you follow this rule you are not nearly so likely to drive off down the road with both tanks bouncing merrily around

PREPARING FOR THE ROAD

or (as has happened many times) bouncing independently down the highway on their own. A much more common, and somewhat less catastrophic result is the breakage of the pin which holds the bottom of the support mast in place. When the latter happens you get to bring both bottles up in the car with you until you can find someone to weld a new pin in place.

If you are going to be operating in cold weather (anything under 40 degrees F.) you will want the 'all-weather' hose. The type I use is identifiable by a rectangular rubber binding wound helixically around the basic hose structure. Some types of plastic hose that are not 'all-weather' will break, if bent, in cold weather. On Christmas Eve morning, when you've just arrived at your holiday location and are hooking up (with all trailer outfitting stores closed for the long weekend) this casualty can be discouraging.

Water Hose — Item 15: In stowing your fresh water hose it is well to be very sure to get all the dirt or sand off both fittings and then, after coiling, mate the two. It takes only a small particle of foreign material or a grain of sand, lodged in just the right place, to make your one-way stop-valve inoperative — then the water you have placed in your tank proceeds to leak out while you travel blithly down the road. That evening when you stop for the night (in the desert, no doubt) you (and someone else) are likely to be somewhat less than satisfied with the situation. Of course you can get by on the few gallons you carry in plastic jugs (if you're smart) for just such unforseen emergencies.

Sanitator — Item 18: Many an unpleasant episode could be related concerning the inadvertent neglect to close the holding tank (sanitator) dump-valve. This can happen anytime you dump. You may be in a hurry and doing several things at once so it just slips your mind (it probably won't more than once, because of the severe jolt your memory will get when you become aware) and away you go.

While we're on the subject of dumping, be reminded that a holding tank should always be used as a holding tank and not as a thru discharge. If you leave the dump valve open during continued use, while connected to a sewer, the outlet is likely to get fouled by toilet tissue so that when the dump-valve is closed is will force the tissue into its groove. After a few layers of tissue get crammed into the groove the fitting is no longer watertight, and you have a problem.

However, in the event you have already gotten yourself into this pickle, or perhaps because of a failure to flush out adequately after dumping, paper is caught in the groove there is a treatment, short of surgery back at the certified service center, which will usually dislodge the impediment — if it hasn't been packed in too firmly. In any event it should certainly be worth a try.

Here is the procedure. Dump and rinse the Sanitator thor-

PREPARING FOR THE ROAD

oughly. Close the outside waste terminal by using the cover provided. Place five gallons of water in the Sanitator tank along with one dose of Pink Magic or TST. **Leave the dump-valve open.** Proceed to your next overnight stop without using the Sanitator (or drive over some uneven terrain and around a few corners for an hour). Drain the Sanitator by removing the waste terminal cover (the dump-valve can be partially closed for this maneuver to forestall misfortune, but **do not close completely.**) Flush the Sanitator tank with four or five full water closets of water. Try your dump valve. If it does not seat all the way without forcing (as can be told by the dump handle's position with respect to the hold down clips) go thru the procedure once more. The smaller quantity of five gallons is used to encourage the flow of water back and forth thru the dump valve. Also there will be less soiling of the bathtub. The latter can be avoided if you will procure an adjustable "Snap-Tite" bathtub stopper (carried by Wally Byam stores).

"Here is the Snap-Tite bath-tub stopper, useful in keeping waste water from backing up into the tub when you want to use your drain lines as a wash-water depositor temporarily, or when leaving your dump valve open for cleaning it."

PREPARING FOR THE ROAD

Wheel Lugs — Item 21: I frequently read admonitions to check wheel lugs for tightness before every departure. Where there is so much smoke maybe there is some fire — but I'm not sure. I haven't personally met anyone who has lost a wheel that way. And I can't help wondering why lugs should back off on trailer wheels any quicker than on automobile wheels. A bit of assurance can be had by going over the lugs with a standard 27" lug wrench (the kind that is furnished with your automobile). This additional leverage will improve on the job done by the typical "T" wrench used by tire-repair facilities by a good part of a turn.

However, if you wish to heed the warning I suggest you leave your hub caps at home so you can check the lugs at a glance at each stop. Many people are convinced that hub caps add nothing, esthetically, to the appearance of a travel trailer. A more streamlined look is gained by eliminating them entirely, particularly on aluminum clad trailers. Thus forty or fifty dollars could be saved.

Pilots — Item 22: You are probably wondering why, if the refrigerator is to be kept lighted, one should be so concerned with turning all the others off. As I see it, if there are two flames in the trailer and one goes out leaving raw gas entering the trailer (assuming the thermal safety switch didn't function) **the remaining flame will probably ignite the escaped gas** — and produce some new vents where they aren't wanted. If there is no other flame present there is little liklihood of ignition. Smelly, yes. But dangerous only if you go in with a lighted cigaret to look for the leak.

Some of us leave our appliances on, anyway, if they will stay on and providing they serve a purpose (the furnace in very cold weather, the hot-water for convenience) choosing to exercise our confidence in the safety cut-off provisions (thermal valves) and thereby achieve the greater convenience. However, under no circumstances should any appliance be left on which does not have a thermal safety valve. The Magic Chef oven pilot, for instance, falls in this category — it is manually operated.

Refrigerator — Item 31: Many refrigerators tend to quit functioning as soon as the trailer starts moving along at highway speeds. The burner flame is extinguished by air draft through the ventilating opening the trailer floor under the refrigerator. The simplest, surest and most economical way to prevent this is to place a fairly heavy, flexible pad over the aperature while travelling. A piece of rubber floor tile, foam rubber rug padding, or rubber door mat. However, the cover must be removed when parked in warm weather — or the refrigerator will not work.

While we are discussing preparation for the road it might be well to mention an inexpensive aid that will take a lot of the

"The "keeper of the peace". Use a 6" convex mirror (this one is a Vel-Vac) mounted on the jack post to enable you to back your hitch ball smartly under the hitch coupler every time on the first try."

PREPARING FOR THE ROAD

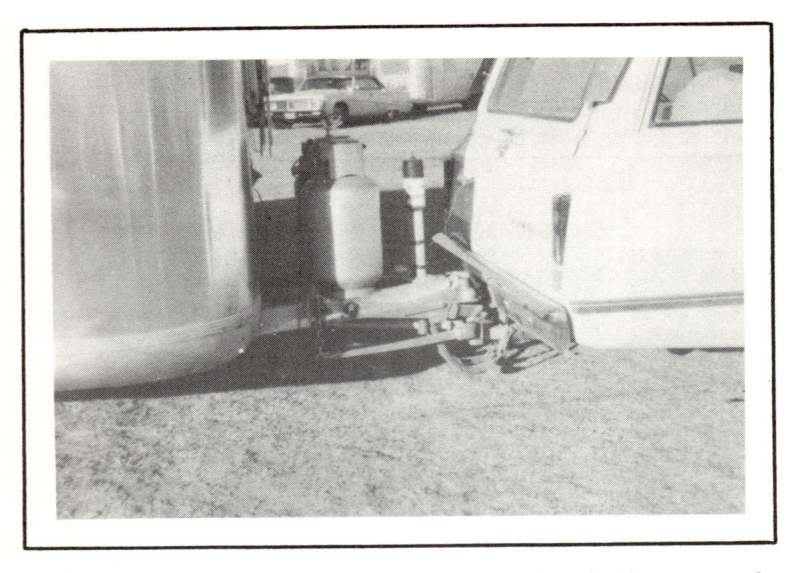

If you don't trust your backing finesse (or your wife's signals) you can always have a collision bar welded to the ball mount, as shown here, to absorb the contact.

friction (between members of the party) out of hooking up. If you haven't seen the typical scene at hook-up time, with the driver behind the wheel trying to place the hitch ball under a 2" cap, by backing his tow vehicle, while his wife stands guard at the trailer tongue and directs him with indefinite, erratic but none the less emphatic gestures as she repeatedly coaches the ball into any position but the right one — then you haven't been initiated. Many flared tempers can be spared, much blood pressure eliminated, if you will spend two dollars for an inexpensive mirror head (replacement unit) at a trailer supply house, and mount the thing over your hitch. Mounting can be very simple. Pick up two 12" lengths of aluminum tubing, one of slightly smaller diameter than the other, from a junk pile or at a hobby shop. Secure the larger one parallel to and in front of the trailer jack shaft just behind the hitch cap with a hose clamp. Flatten one end of the other piece of tubing, drill a 1/4" hole in the flattened end and mount the mirror head on it. Then bend the tubing to about a 30 degree angle and drop the unbent portion into the larger tubing which you have secured to the trailer jack shaft. Presto. You have a perfect view of your ball placement operation and you can put it into exact position on the very first try — leaving the wife to attend to titivating the interior of the trailer, and in full possession of her temper.

PREPARING FOR THE ROAD

    For just another dollar a 6" convex mirror (the smaller ones won't do) can be had that will increase your visual field several times. This makes the positioning of the mirror less critical and places your hitch ball in view at a greater distance from the coupler, allowing you to correct your position from further away as you back in. Also, due to the wider lateral field of vision, placement of the mirror head in its slot is less critical.

CHECK-OFF LIST For Departure

Exterior:
1. Keeper in hitch pin?
2. Safety pin in ball latch?
3. Equalizer bar chain-lifts latched?
4. Safety chains attached?
5. Safety brake cable attached?
6. 7-Way electric cable plugged in all circuits working?
7. Gas bottles secured snugly?
8. Rock shield stowed?
9. Windows closed and latched?
10. Radio antenna stowed?
11. TV antenna stowed?
12. Holding tank dumped?
13. Sewer hose cleaned and stowed?
14. Power cord stowed and lead-out cover secured?
15. Fresh water hose stowed?
16. Runner blocks and chocks picked up and stowed?
17. All exterior compartment doors locked?
18. Holding tank dump-valve closed?
19. Door mat stowed?
20. Door step secured?
21. Wheel lugs tight?
22. Tires inflated properly?
23. Extension mirrors in place?
24. Refrigerator vent cover in place?

Interior:
26. Oven pilot valve closed?
27. All compartment doors and covers latched?
28. Water pump off?
29. Windows closed and latched?
30. All loose items secured? Separate list may be in order.
31. Refrigerator pin in door?

Chapter 6

RECOMMENDED DRIVING TECHNIQUES FOR TOWING TRAILERS

First a basic principle must be accepted — that towing a heavy trailer is not the same as driving an unhampered automobile. Once this is firmly established as an unalterable and heavily burdened fact the rest is simply a matter of mastering a few techniques that accept that principle and all that it involves, and you're ready for the road. It is assumed that you have followed the guidelines laid out in the chapter on Unit Harmony and have a properly engineered rig to begin with, recognizing that the best driver on the road will still be a danger to himself and others if he moves onto a highway with an unsafe unit. Driving techniques are discussed in the following paragraphs in their estimated order of importance.

Passing

Allow more distance for acceleration and for passing — about two to one. You can do somewhat better if you push it, but it will cost you — a lot more gas, and greater repair costs. For example, universal joints are subjected to greater strain, and fail much quicker, when high torque is applied to the rear wheels thereby forcing the rear axle housing to rotate forward and downward. In fact, maximum torque subjects the entire drive train to greater stress (hence liklihood of failure) than does normal torque.

Be sure there is enough room for your trailer when returning to your original lane after passing, but don't delay unnecessarily. I find that the instant the other vehicle passes from view in my inside rearview mirror is exactly the right time to move back in lane.

Stopping

Allow more time for deceleration and for stopping. Although you have brakes on all six (or eight) wheels they may not synchronize as well as the four you are accustomed to. Also, the inertial force which each car wheel is called upon to arrest, due to the hitch weight now on the tow vehicle, may be considerably greater than that for which the brakes were designed. The same goes for the trailer brakes if the trailer is heavily loaded.

DRIVING TECHNIQUES

Clearance

Allow more clearance — for parking, for turns, for drive thru, and for overhead objects. And **keep checking** as you maneuver. **Know** that you are in the clear. Don't guess. Remember that damaged trailer body usually requires several times as long to repair as a car body, and costs more. So have someone get out and watch the rear or the blind side, or get out as many times as necessary, yourself, to insure that you are clear. When backing your rig, **always** have someone watching out for anything that may develop behind you. I have started backing, a time or two, when completely off the road and out in the country, only to find that some innocent driver had pulled directly in behind me. Also have someone watch the rear of your trailer when making hard turns — the rear swings way wide of the wheel tracks, especially in the longer models (26' and up).

Entering Freeways

When pulling onto a busy, high speed freeway or highway use maximum acceleration. This is one time when the interests of safety demand the sacrifice of fuel and heavier stress on working parts, as in passing.

Cruising Speed

Keep your cruising speed down. Most states limit the speed for towed vehicles to 45 or 50 MPH, which is really only prudent. A towing rig can't possibly be as maneuverable as a single vehicle operating at the same speed. In fact, I have never known of a single trailer catastrophe (with no other vehicle involved) at a speed under 45 MPH, except where the driver fell asleep or suffered an attack of some kind.

Begin to recognize and appreciate the increased visibility and the awareness of your surroundings which you enjoy while travelling at lower speeds.

Downhill Driving

Use lower gears for descending grades. The rule is for 'minimum braking'. Here it is assumed that you followed the earlier rule that demands a 'lock-in' type automatic transmission for just such situations. If road and traffic conditions warrant 50 MPH or less, take the grade in 2nd and keep your speed braked down to not more than 50. If road and traffic conditions warrant 30 MPH or less, take the grade in 1st and keep your speed braked down to not more than 30. Usually, when traffic signs warn trucks to 'use lower gear' this warrants 1st gear for your rig. Good idea to start the grade that way, anyway — you can always shift up. Remember that with most transmissions you have to be going less than 30 for the transmission to shift into 1st, even though you select 1st gear manually.

DRIVING TECHNIQUES

When braking on long grades, hold brakes on only for brief intervals to avoid fading. Once they start fading you are in serious trouble. In this respect, avoid having your brakes relined with cheaper linings — they are much more subject to fading when hot. Also you want to avoid starting the descent of a mountain range involving several thousands of feet with very low batteries as the generator or alternator may not be able to supply the trailer brakes at idling speed. This could be especially hazardous if your tow vehicle was equipped with a non lock-in type transmission and generator (low idling charge rate) in lieu of alternator.

Uphill Driving

Use lower gears for climbing grades to avoid overheating and engine strain. When car speed decreases to 50 at full throttle, shift to 2nd gear. Do not exceed 50 in 2nd. When car speed decreases to 30, shift to 1st gear. Do not exceed 30 in 1st.

Be aware of overtaking traffic on grades so that you may use 'pull-outs' and wide shoulders to allow fast traffic to pass. When operating a slow vehicle this is a duty as well as a safety policy. However, avoid carrying this practice to such extremes that you pull out when your own rig is endangered, such as when climbing under full power an usually steep grade and the length of the pull-out looks short, unless you are prepared to come to a full stop if necessary.

Traffic Behind You

Be aware of vehicles behind you at all times. This is particularly important for a towing vehicle because of the extra length and the decreased mobility. I use fender-mount mirrors for constant surveillance and the car's factory mounted outside mirrors for the areas outside of the fender-mounted mirror's field of vision, on either side. I still take a quick look to the side by a turn of the head before moving either to the right or to the left, just in case someone has escaped my vision by pulling into passing position from an access lane or driveway.

Curves

Take all curves either under power or at greatly reduced speed — on down grade not more than half the speed at which you would normally take the same curve in an unburdened automobile. When you are in a curve with power off, especially on a down grade, your tow is exerting hundreds of pounds of inertia centrifugally — toward the outside of the curve — and all of that force is applied to your hitch point, again with a leverage factor (due to the distance the hitch is positioned behind the rear axle) acting to move your rear wheels to the outside of the curve. This physical phenomenon can't be ignored, unless you want to

DRIVING TECHNIQUES

pay a price. Here is part of the justification for carrying more weight on your rear axle than might otherwise be necessary, and for inflating the tires to greater pressure — the side thrust will almost force an underinflated tire off the rim.

Overheating

Avoid overheating engine or transmission. An engine that is subjected to overheating develops sludge which increases the tendency to overheat. Also, burned valves frequently result. Overheating a transmission is likely to burn the fluid, which then contaminates the seals and deposits carbon in the fluid lines, valves and pumps, and may cause clutch bands to disintegrate.

Any time overheating is suspected it is a good idea to inspect the crankcase oil and transmission fluid. If the former is black and dirty, replace. If the latter is anything but clear and red (like new fluid) replace it. In replacing transmission fluid all of the fluid should be drained, including that which remains in the torque converter (removed by separate drain plug), and the filter should be removed and cleaned. This necessitates removal of the bottom cover plate which should be removed and cleaned anyway.

If repeated overheating of the transmission occurs, as shown by burned fluid, perhaps an auxiliary transmission cooler should be installed. For additional information on the use of an auxiliary cooler refer to Chapter 3.

However, before resorting to other measures, it might be a good idea to examine your driving techniques. Are you shifting to lower gears on inclines to keep your RPM engine up? This results in a greater rate of circulation, hence greater cooling, of transmission fluid, radiator coolant and fan-driven air — the latter, of course, only if you have a direct-drive fan rather than the silicone clutch type which cuts out at higher engine speeds (refer to Chapter 3).

Are you idling your engine for several moments when you stop, in order to dissipate the heat that has developed under load in the engine block, crankcase oil and transmission? Remember that the transmission fluid circulation pump, as well as engine oil and coolant continue to be recirculated and are cooled while the engine idles. The engine temperature gauge will at first show a sharp rise, which is because the pumps and fan, at idling speed, aren't as effective and because air velocity, added by forward movement, is gone. Shortly, however, the engine and transmission heat will be largely dissipated and the engine can be stopped without undue heat build-up. This build-up, if not avoided, will sometimes 'blow-off' either radiator coolant, transmission fluid, or both. Especially when you have been in hard pull, in hot weather, for a long time. In extreme cases it is well to sit with the transmission in neutral and the engine held at a fast idle for a minute or two before slowing to a normal idle.

"Tow vehicles original outside mirror deflected to increase field of vision — makes visible any auto already in passing position."

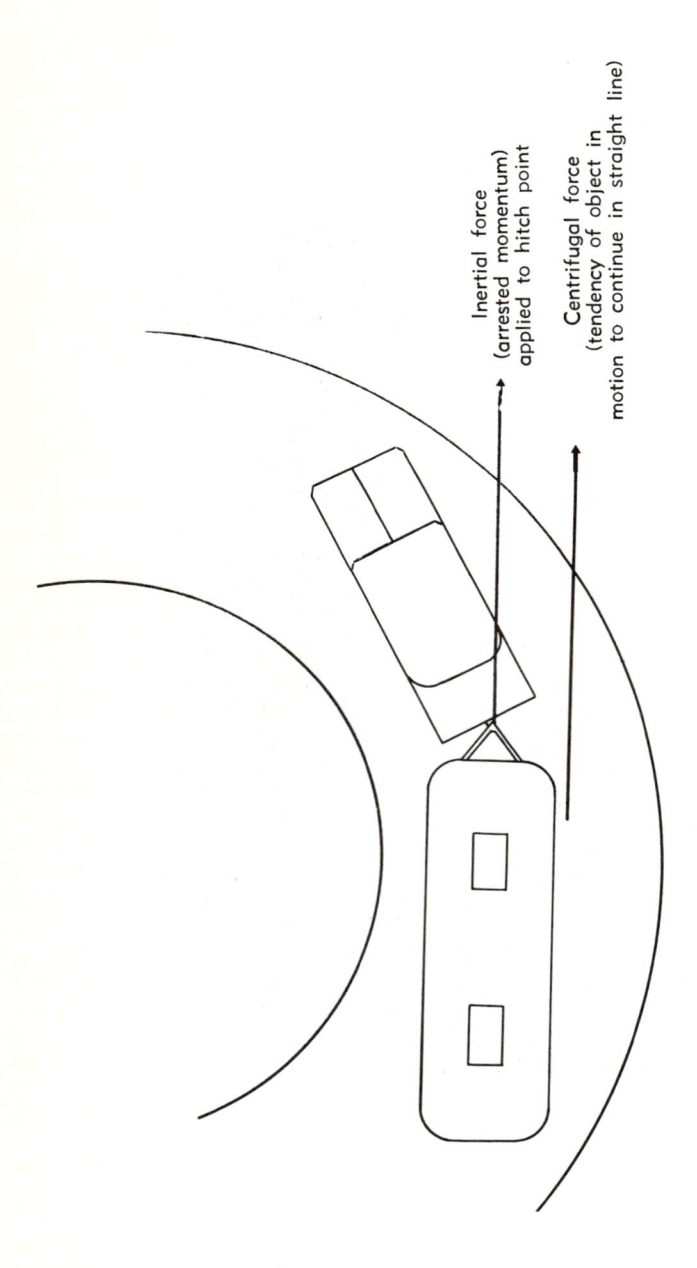

Inertial force
(arrested momentum)
applied to hitch point

Centrifugal force
(tendency of object in
motion to continue in straight line)

Sketch illustrates inertial thrust exerted on rear of tow vehicle, when holding trailer back, toward outside of curve, in addition to normal centrifugal force.

DRIVING TECHNIQUES

Do not idle your engine with the transmission engaged as this will result in even greater temperature rise. Circulation of the fluid is maintained by engine RPM and has nothing to do with whether or not the transmission is engaged. Are you stopping at "view points" while climbing steep grades? The maximum power that must be expended to get moving again generates a terrific amount of heat — and at the time when no air velocity is being generated by forward movement. Make a practice of catching the view-points on the way down.

Are you maintaining all fluid and coolant reservoirs at the 'full' mark? If they are low this condition contributes to over-heating. In this respect, however, let me caution against over-filling the transmission. Even a little extra fluid can cause the transmission fluid to blow-off when extremely hot — and draw the fluid level down below the minimum required (usually first detected by a refusal of the transmission to shift gears, or by delayed shift). The same phenomenon can occur to the radiator coolant, also. In checking transmission fluid level, check with engine idling and only when the transmission is thoroughly warmed up, preferably after several hours of towing, and be sure you seat the dip-stick well into the filler tube when taking a reading. You may have to try several times to get a clear reading on the dip stick due to the oil dripping onto the stick because of turbulance. **Do not** let service station attendants check your transmission fluid level. Check it yourself. It circulates in a sealed system and, unless there is a gasket leak or it is over-heating and blowing out the vent pipe, the level of fluid will remain constant between changes (usually recommended at twenty to thirty thousand mile intervals). I keep a small plastic jar filled with new fluid and when the fluid in use becomes appreciably darker in color than that in the jar I have the fluid changed. Due to the extra heavy duty to which my transmission is put, towing a double load, I've had to change as often as four thousand (in the Rocky Mountains) and as infrequently as twenty thousand.

A substantial rise in the level of fluid from previous readings is sufficient cause to take your vehicle in for a check up. Air bubbles on the dip stick would indicate aeration from a leaky pump. No bubbles but a high reading would indicate a clogged filter preventing normal flow into the torque converter — hence the build up in the transmission. In any case, an examination now may save you many dollars later if you let the situation go unheeded.

An emergency procedure that can help keep the engine temperature down involves the utilization of air-conditioning system and heating system for cooling the engine. The first time I tried this we were crossing the desert into Las Vegas on a hot day (110 degrees official). We were climbing steadily and the

DRIVING TECHNIQUES

engine temperature kept mounting. As the needle approached the danger mark I shifted from 2nd down to 1st, reducing speed to 30 MPH, then 15. The needle held for a while then started to drift upward again. Next I switched off the air conditioner, opening all windows. Again the needle held for a time then started inexorably upward. In desperation I turned the heat control full on, holding my breath as I watched the needle. This time it steadied, then backed off a notch — and held, all the way to the top (Black Mountain). Just that small amount of added radiator capacity — contained in the heating unit — saved the day. Of course we got pretty warm! But no more so than we would have sitting alongside the highway.

Of some interest was the number of other rigs stalled alongside the highway. After a while we got to counting them — my wife's diary entry shows 23, and there must have been as many more before we started counting. Many were campers and trailer tows, but some were late model automobiles with no tow. Some, I'm sure(had stopped simply because the temperature gauge showed 'hot'. In such a situation as we were in I wouldn't consider stopping unless the needle went all the way. A modern automobile can withstand a lot of heat without suffering any damage as long as the coolant is retained and the motor is kept turning over. But of course if you have an automobile equipped with only an 'idiot light' as a source of information, and that comes on — you have no choice but to stop. Let's be optimistic and assume that you followed the recommendations included in Chapter 3, and had a meter installed.

A transmission is frequently overheated (and sometimes damaged) after the trip is over. If you have just finished a long grade, or a hard run, when you arrive at your destination let your engine and transmission cool before doing any 'backing and filling' to get set up for the day in the camp site of your choice. Let the engine sit and idle while you scout around and find your spot — unless its merely a matter of pulling straight in and stopping. Even a short haul in reverse to back onto your runner blocks can be the proverbial straw. If the transmission fluid comes foaming out the overflow and onto the ground — you'll know you lost your gamble.

Fish Tailing (Weaving)

If, in spite of your sway control device, your streamlined trailer, and the harmonious relationship which you have designed into your unit, you ever do find your trailer fishtailing wildly — out of control, it can usually be brought back under control providing you do the correct thing and do it quickly enough. Just depress the accelerator all the way to the stop (but not far enough to engage the passing-gear switch because you can't afford the second or two it takes for the transmission to shift down) and

DRIVING TECHNIQUES

shove the trailer brake hand control full on. In most cases, however severe, this will straighten the unit out instantly. As soon as your tow is tracking again, release the trailer brakes and proceed on your way. Trailing a WMCC buddy on the turnpike between Cuernavaca and Mexico City I watched his trailer go into oscillation as he passed a slow moving truck at about 70 MPH (he had speeded up to get around quickly) so badly that I could see first one side and then the other of both tow car and trailer. Remembering the briefing given us at one of George Dey's driver meetings, he applied the correction described above and presto! — tracking right on down the highway. Left a few dollars worth of rubber on the pavement but saved fifteen thousand in rolling stock.

Seat Belts

I have personally witnessed two, and had first hand accounts of several more, accidents resulting in upset of both tow vehicle and trailer. In all instances the passengers received only minor, if any, injury. I'm sure this can be attributed to two factors. First, the inertia of a ten to twelve thousand pound rig, and second, the value of seat belts. In all these instances seat belts were worn. In Mexico I watched a Plymouth/Tradewind unit (24 ft.) fishtail itself over on its back and skid fifty feet down the highway — only to see the driver and passenger unfasten their seat belts and come crawling out the windows, upside down, without a scratch! This appears to be the rule rather than the exception. Incidentally this particular driver had set his trailer brake manual adjustment so as to eliminate 'grabbing' in city traffic, and then had forgotten to reset it. Hence he had almost no trailer brakes available from the brake pedal — and he didn't think to operate the control by hand. The fellow who expects to depend on using the hand control in an emergency is a dreamer — in a real emergency he is likely to find both hands full of steering wheel just to keep heading in the right direction and his foot will already, by driver's reflex, be hard down on the brake pedal. So you'd better have the trailer brakes set up to function, in proper proportion, automatically.

Sleeping Sickness

I call this sleeping sickness because if you allow yourself to get drowsy at the wheel of an automobile, tow or no tow, you're sick — in the head. This sort of accident happens daily among trailerists and it comes closest to being unforgivable. You've got your bed with you so why not just pull over and take a comfortable nap? Or have a cup of coffee? And it can happen to anyone. A close friend of mine, who has towed a trailer for years and covered many thousands of miles without even a minor accident with one, went soundly to sleep at 45 MPH, and simply

DRIVING TECHNIQUES

ran off the road — and rolled over and over. The trailer was a total loss, the Continental almost so. Don't wait for the first droop of the eyelids — stop when they first begin to get a little heavy, or your eyes drift out of focus, or you find yourself less aware of things around you. You may not be so lucky as my friend. He suffered a bruised back — his wife a bruised shin. Both wore seat belts, of course. Do you suppose he and his wife were getting tired of fastening those seat belts day after day, all for nothing?

Backing

Learn to back your trailer proficiently. The one thing that marks you as a competent trailerist is to be able to back your trailer expertly into place, whether in a mobile home park, a nature park slot or a rally spot. You didn't begrudge the time spent learning to back your car into the curb so that you could obtain a driver's license — so treat this capability the same way. A good idea is to find an almost deserted shopping center parking lot — Sundays are perfect — and practice backing into marked off spaces from all angles. In short order you can become adept at backing your trailer into spaces on your left. Spaces on your right will take some time, and you can never learn to hit them regularly the first try, unassisted. Next learn to back your trailer in a straight line. You will use this capability countless times. It is simply a matter of learning to line up the left side of your trailer in your left hand extension mirror and to keep it lined up, with small movements of the wheel, while you continue backing at slow speed. I once had to back out of a single lane, dead-end street for almost half a mile. I was glad I had gotten in some practice when I didn't **have** to back it.

Sandy Going

Years ago I ventured off a county road into an arroyo to make my way down to the Colorado river, towing a 14 ft. Sportsman. I made it to the river without any problem — it was down grade. But when I attempted to return to the highway the next morning I couldn't get any traction in the sand. Upgrade I couldn't move.

In somewhat of a panic as we had run out of food and water (the Colorado was muddy) I forgot everything I had learned about getting out of snow banks and ice traps in New England and hied myself out to the roadway to get help. In about an hour a rancher came along in a pickup and stopped at my frantic arm waving. Upon hearing me describe my predicament he brusquely advised me to "let the air out of your rear tires and come on out — you won't have any trouble." Whereupon, he drove off without further ado. Naturally I kicked myself all the way back to the rig — because I had used just this technique many times to get out of ice and snow — but I wasn't smart enough to apply

DRIVING TECHNIQUES

it to sand! I even had a compression pump (screws into the cylinder head in place of a spark plug, available at Montgomery Wards) with me for restoring the tires to the proper air pressure once I got out. And, just like the man said, after lowering the pressure to about ten pounds I came right out, trailer and all.

With your trailer you have another ace up your sleeve. If you can't get traction try dropping part, (or all) of your hitch weight onto the rear axle. Be sure you do this **before** you've burried your wheels or you will simply set body down on to the ground. One or both of the above tricks will usually move you. If not — jack up the wheels and put on the chains, or get some boards. I also keep a bag of Cat Litter in the trunk when I'm operating in snow or ice — it acts like sand and will extract you from some minor situations, like getting away from a curb, etc.

Stationary Steering

Avoid turning your steering wheel with the car stationary, when hitch weight is on, especially if your front tires are a little soft. The extra weight demands so much more force that pressure hoses are frequently ruptured and seals sometimes displaced.

Night Driving

Avoid driving at night when practicable. Night driving is estimated to be about twice as hazardous as daytime driving, other things being equal, and with your somewhat unwieldy rig it becomes even more so. Why miss all the scenery on your way — isn't that why you are traveling? If you do plan to drive nights I suggest you have the front and rear cluster lights installed above the front and rear windows. Trucks are required to be equipped with these and some states, New Jersey for one, require them on travel trailers.

These lights serve warning to approaching vehicles that you **are** a big, heavy, unwieldy vehicle — and they can be expected to use a bit more caution in their approach — who wants to run into a seventy ton gasoline tanker? And the other driver has no choice but to assume that you may very well be one.

Chapter 7
MAINTENANCE AND REPAIR

Much of the routine maintenance and repair required on your travel trailer can be performed by you, with the proper tools and a little initiative. A number of items that are common to many trailers are described below. A tool list, the possession of which will enable you to tackle the work outlined plus many auto repairs, will be found at the end of the chapter.

Door Locks

Door locks get difficult to operate — keys fail to slide in and out easily or locks become difficult to turn. Give them a shot of dry lubricant (CRC 5-56 at auto parts stores; Spra-Kleen at Wally Byam Stores; Elmers Slide-All at hardware and auto accessory stores). Once freed up, a shot of dry graphite will help keep them that way.

Gas Bottles

Be sure the gas bottles are tightened in place snugly at all times when travelling. Loose tanks sometimes result in a sheared pin at the bottom of the retainer rod and in fractures developing around the tank input fitting on the pig-tail. A spare pig-tail, incidentally, is a good item for your spare-parts kit.

Hitch

Apply a little ball lubricant to hitch ball and to compensator bars at all contact points (both head and chain). Without adequate lubrication the bars will wear out of fit at the head, and the bottom and top links in the chain will eventually wear through. When a chain lets go while moving you'll think you've just exploded a land mine.

Hub Caps

Some of the larger hub caps have a tendency to rotate within the wheel rim, forcing the valve stem down under the hub cap. Some of them are shaken loose and go rolling away. On making

MAINTENANCE AND REPAIR

a U-turn at a Bull Shoals observation point last summer I encountered one lying in the road. I picked it up and hung it on the wall of the overlook shelter so that the unfortunate loser could find it easily when he returned to look for it. Upon parking for the night, some two hundred miles south, I discovered it was my own hub cap hanging back there on the wall. Oh, well. A new one cost me only twelve dollars or so.

I picked up a tip from another trailerist, later. As he suggested, I rolled a strip of 1½" masking tape lengthwise, sticky side out, and fitted it between the rim and the hub cap on all four wheels (these are the hub caps that secure to the **rim** of the wheel (on '65 Airstream, etc.) rather than to the hub). For twenty months and forty thousand miles they remained plastered to the rim. Whatever else untoward may have happened I still had by big beautiful hub caps. The new models don't have that trouble — but I've decided I don't like hub caps anyway so I stored the new ones. If hub caps were made optional equipment many purchasers would save themselves forty or fifty dollars — watch the denuded trailers go by and you'll agree that people must not care for them.

Exterior Finish

My Airstream has a coating of clear plastic (Macrylic, I believe) over the polished aluminum. Those areas of the finish that have suffered only the rigors of weather — temperatures ranging from −10 to 120, hail, wind, cloudburst, dust, mud and sand) looked just like they did two years earlier. But, like so many venturesome types (that's my name for it — my wife spells it 'reckless') I keep pushing tree limbs and briars out of the way with my trailer — and these obstacles just will leave their mark. Also large Texas size bugs (as well as the larger ones, Alaska-bred) when striking the front of the trailer at sixty MPH will pit the plastic somewhat, presumably more by chemical action than force if you don't scrub them off right away. My post-game quarterbacking would call for careful avoidance of all objects, both animate and inanimate. I would say, off-hand, that ten feet interval would be about right.

Frequent washing with cold water (and a mild auto soap) is recommended for washing bugs, as well as dirt, off the finish. Being frugal with my labor, I wash mine at the 25c car wash booths that utilize hot water and auto detergent. I get a good cleaning for a dollar (two full cycles for rinsing — one for the top alone) and at the end of two years could find no signs of damage to the Macrylic.

However, for day to day 'freshening', I use a good quality chemically-treated dust cloth, and get only as high as I can reach. A coat of Simoniz Wax applied occasionally facilitates the dust removing operation.

MAINTENANCE AND REPAIR

Brakes

After thirty thousand miles of travel, quite a bit of it on wet roads, my trailer brakes began to grab and then release alternately when applied, resulting in an up-and-down oscillation at the hitch that threatened to break up house-keeping (both literally and figuratively). It was not noticeable at high speeds but under twenty MPH it became increasingly severe.

I did not then have an ohm-meter with me or I could have determined the trouble in a few minutes. I have since corrected that deficiency with a small, but effective volt-ohm meter which I think no trailer buff should be without. Even if you are not versed in electrical circuitry you can do very well with the amateur type — they come with a set of simple instructions. At under $8.00 mine is Japanese made, but competitive U.S. versions will not be long in making their appearance. A common automobile type ammeter is useful, also, for trouble shooting 12-volt circuits and appliances.

As it happened, I drove a harrowing two thousand miles or more before a fellow caravanner, with whom I had earlier made the WBCC '65 summer Caravan to Alaska, happened into a service station in Forks, Washington, at the same time I did and, in the ensuing exchange of travel news, tipped me off as to the cause of my trouble. As it happened he and several others had suffered the same experience. I just hadn't yet talked to the right people.

Before my fortunate meeting with my friend I had repeatedly flushed out the 7-way plug (with my dry-lube), cleaned line terminals in the tow vehicle and trailer, cleaned and adjusted 7-way terminals, traced the brake lead all the way from motor compartment to the trailer terminal strip, tried various adjustments of the brake resistance panel and the brake control rheostat, and spent considerable effort dodging my wife's barbed remarks concerning the possibility that my opinion of my general competence had, for some time, been somewhat over rated. The trouble lay in the splice at each brake. Although Airstream had selected the best wire nut available for a weather splice, one with a vinyl sleeve that fitted around the wires, water had eventually worked its way down to the twisted strands and corroded them thoroughly. Obviously at least one of the four splices was breaking connection (electrically) on each initial surge of the trailer braking operation and then remaking connection as the springs recovered (or vice versa).

Even in the older models I'm sure this is not a common trouble, but one that can occur if the trailer is towed through a lot of water. Accordingly, I wouldn't recommend any preventive measure — just be prepared to recognize the source of trouble when, and if, it is encountered. A poor connection elsewhere

MAINTENANCE AND REPAIR

might produce the same effect but I strongly doubt it. I think the fact that many very small strands of corroded wire were twisted together made this phenomenon possible.

Two other, rather common, sources of brake circuit trouble result from damage suffered to the 7-way cable where it is led back through the A-frame channel (sometimes ruptured by rivets, sometimes burned by welding operations — during either construction or repairs) and from poorly placed "lead-through" grommets in the skin, leading to the solenoids.

Wheel Bearings

If the wheel bearings have been packed properly with either Automotive Multi-Purpose Grease or Wheel Bearing Lubricant— Medium, they should not require repacking until the brakes require relining. The recommendation, when made by trailer manufacturers that they be repacked every 10,000 miles would indicate that some less durable lubricant may have been used initially. If you are confronted with this recommendation I would certainly follow it — the first time. But at 10,000 miles, when I had them repacked, I would insist on one of the above lubricants being used. These lubricants are good for as long as they remain in place. After that, you need only check the bearing for excessive play at the 10,000 mile intervals, re-greasing the bearings only when brake linings need replacing, or at 30,000 mile intervals for peace-of-mind.

Lack of lubricant, or too snug an adjustment, will sometimes cause wheel bearings to overheat. If overheating is suspected, simply feel the wheel rim and the tire with your hand and compare with the others — assuming they are inflated equally. A difference of more than a few degrees will spell trouble.

Body Steel

The steel trailer frame and gas bottles (and rack) need to be coated with a rust inhibiting aluminum paint, as the factory coat of material is likely to be very thin, and sometimes may be enamel bearing the phrase "anti-rust", meaning merely that it will adhere to **clean** metal surfaces closely enough to prevent the entry of oxygen (hence preventing rust). All of the latter with which I am familiar require a 'primer' or rust-inhibiting agent to be effective in preventing rust, as there is almost no such thing as a 'clean' metal surface.

A going over with a wire brush, followed with a good spray coat of the aluminum (metal) paint usually serves to keep and preserve the surfaces for many months.

Battery

My '65 Airstream was equipped with a so-called "Uni-Volt" system whereby the trailer utilities (lights, furnace, etc.) operate on 12-volts only, with a converter furnishing the 12 volts from a

MAINTENANCE AND REPAIR

110 volt input when plugged into utility power, simultaneously charging the trailer battery if it needs charging. This system eliminates the old procedure of switching all the trailer circuits over each time you changed power sources, and also provides a fully charged battery the next time you start out on the road — without any thinking or effort on your part. It just happens.

However, occasionally you might hook up to a higher-than-normal power voltage and find your battery overcharging. When this happened the electrolyte would boil (called 'gassing') and evaporate all of the water in the electrolyte. After losing one battery due to sulfation (nothing left in the battery but hydrochloric acid) I read the instructions and found I could have forestalled this occurance by moving a shorting strap on the Uni-Volt case which thereby increased the number of turns in the primary of the power transformer and hence reduced the charging voltage. I performed the recommended operation and just left it there. In some locations my lights weren't quite so bright as in others but the replacement battery was still good when I sold the trailer. The '68 has an improved Uni-Volt, the Mark III, which is designed to provide a constant output with much greater variation in input voltage. It does not require adjusting.

Although the single battery furnished with the Airstream is good for an overnight stop in **almost** any kind of weather (barring sub-zero) it is not adequate to meet the needs of those of us who find it desirable to spend a considerable part of our time in National and State Parks, and in wilderness areas where there is no public power source available for charging the battery and considering that we sometimes like to leave our trailer set for days while we fish, or hunt, or hike. Nor, for that matter, is it adequate for day to day travel in cold weather where the furnace has to be used most of the night for comfort. For the simple reason that the battery does not receive enough charge in a normal day's driving to meet the needs of a cold night. Let's take a close look at the situation.

Consider a 16 hour lay-over during which time we would need battery power, unassisted by the tow vehicle's charging system, to operate all power accessories. Allowing 36 ampere hours for 4 hours of continuous furnace blower operation at 9 amps per hour ('65 Airstream and a moderately cold night) or 8 hours of operation at 4½ amps per hour ('67 Airstream), 5 ampere-hours water pump operation (1 hr. total), 9 ampere-hours for lights and exhaust fans (kitchen and bathroom) for a total of 50 ampere-hours of power capacity expended. Not bad, eh? Looks like we're in good shape. Away we go to our next destination 8 hours away, when we'll be all charged up again, with 70 ampere-hours ('65) or 90 ampere-hours ('67) of capacity ready to handle the next night's power needs. But wait.

If you will insert an ammeter in the charge line while you go blithely on your high way, you will find only about 2 amps

MAINTENANCE AND REPAIR

flowing to your trailer battery. Eight hours at 2 amps per hour amount to 16 ampere-hours. Add this to the 20 we had left in the '65 or the 40 we had left in the '67 and we're in trouble. Out of juice before morning in the '65 and very nearly so in the '67.

The natural question that arises immediately is "Why only 2 amps when any modern alternator is capable of putting out 35? The answer is two-fold. First, the charge line is probably not larger than #10 wire and there is likely to be forty or fifty feet of it between the alternator and the trailer battery. As the effective voltage trying to force current through that long, relatively high resistance, wire is only part of a volt (the difference in the alternator output voltage and the trailer battery terminal voltage), the resulting current flow is going to be much, much lower than the normal rate of charge the car battery would receive if it were in a similar discharged condition, with charging current flowing thru only a few feet of very large wire (probably #4, four times the size of #10). If the latter is only one-tenth as long as the trailer battery charge line and four times as large looks like we'll have forty times as much resistance or one-fortieth as much current for a given impressed voltage, doesn't it? Exactly. But that is not all. Let us look at the other factor.

The voltage regulator that controls the output of the alternator enters the picture. In order that the car battery will not continue to receive a charge (and consequently suffer over-charging) the regulator simply reduces the alternator (or generator) output when the voltage impressed across its terminals reaches that of a fully charged battery under no load. When either the voltage drops (battery partially discharged) or a current drain begins at the battery terminals the battery voltage drops a few tenths of a volt and the regulator calls on the alternator for more current, to restore the higher voltage condition. If we turn on the headlights the alternator meets the demand, and so on up to the maximum capacity of the alternator. We can get almost the full appliance load through the charge line, but the moment we turn them all off the current going to the trailer battery drops immediately to one or two amps, even when the trailer battery is almost fully discharged, because the car battery is now registering almost as much voltage at the regulator terminals as the normal alternator output voltage, and consequently reducing its output to near zero. Of course, the trailer battery, in a discharged state, will draw some charge off the car battery and thus obtain some recharging effect — hence the 1 or 2 amps.

There are several things that we can do to improve the situation. The first, and easiest, is to provide an emergency battery (a small lightweight one will do) for starting the tow vehicle. This will enable us to leave its battery connected, via the 7-way plug (a 10 ft. extension, using #6 or #8 wire and spare 7-way plug and receptacle, can be made up for use when the car can't be

MAINTENANCE AND REPAIR

"A small, inexpensive battery mounted in temporary fashion in the engine compartment, and connected with Sears battery leads, will enable the trailerist to use tow vehicle battery as well as trailer battery, without concern about being unable to start the motor when ready."

parked immediately in front of the trailer) and thus combat successfully two of the inherent faults of the current situation. First the battery capacity (power) available for use in the trailer will be almost doubled (my car uses a 70 ampere hour battery). Second, and of some significance, the car battery will now discharge along with the trailer battery, affording us a maximum charge (thru its influence on the voltage-regulator) when we start out again. Of course, the auto battery will charge up long before the trailer battery will and soon reduce the charging rate.

In order to get more charge out of the alternator while it is putting out at a good rate (before the car battery becomes fully charged) we can employ a #4 or #6 stranded conductor all the way from the main D.C. bus of the car to the trailer battery (don't forget to connect thru the 25 amp circuit breaker mounted in the engine compartment) either using a single conductor connector between car and trailer or splicing the heavier wire into the regular charge line on either side of the 7-way connector.

MAINTENANCE AND REPAIR

Another trick you can use to augment the trailer battery charge is to disconnect the ground lead of your car battery from the block as soon as the ammeter shows that it is no longer putting out a full charge (the engine will have to be left running, of course). This will throw control of the alternator to the trailer battery and the higher charging rate will be maintained as long as it is needed. I have another 7-ampere-hour battery mounted alongside my trailer battery, in the same compartment and connected in parallel with it to its terminal strip, and I am able to get a full charge on all three batteries in five or six hours of driving time, by this maneuver.

If you are going to be parked somewhere for several days and will be using your tow vehicle for daily trips, sight seeing or what not, you can make even better use of your emergency starting battery. After you've plugged in your 7-way connector for the night, lift one end of one of the trailer battery fuses. This will put the trailer load on the car battery and it will be subsequently recharged the next day while you're driving around. The emergency battery can be used to start the car in the event the car battery becomes discharged, thus taking all the risk out of this maneuver. In this way the trailer battery has only to provide power required during the day and should last almost indefinitely, except in very cold weather.

Many people have a gas light installed in the living/eating area, as a further means of conserving electrical power. We have one and have used it to tremendous advantage in some situations. The heat given off by a gas lamp almost eliminates the need for furnace in mildly cold weather and certainly provides enough light for the entire area. Be prepared, however, to install a new mantle anytime you drive over rough roads as you are likely to suffer the loss of the one in use. We've tried 'setting' them with hair spray, and 'isolating' them with plastic bags, when travelling all to no avail. Ours continue to fall apart. But the thirty-five cents or so that one costs can frequently be justified by the advantage gained in its use. In warm weather, the installation and use of one of the new 12-volt, 1 amp, high candle-power fluorescent light fixtures can be justijfied. Enough light can be had for cooking and reading from only one such fixture, and your battery capacity is available for other uses.

A good arrangement for the emergency starting battery is to mount it in the engine compartment, or off to one side of the radiator compartment, and connect it to the block (for ground) and to the auto battery post lug, for starting and for recharging when necessary. Only the ground connection at the block need be removed when it is not in use. Sears has an assortment of replacement battery cables from which you can select the exact lengths you need for making this installation. Besides being much more convenient it assures a good connection, as well as a short

MAINTENANCE AND REPAIR

cable run for starting which you don't always get with battery jumper cables.

Brakes

If you are towing with either a stick shift or a lock-in type automatic transmission your brake linings should last indefinitely. At fifty thousand miles the brakes on my '65 Airstream were less than half gone and the car brakes had just passed another state inspection with original linings and over seventy thousand miles, including fifty towing the trailer. With proper transmission the life of your brake bands depends on driving techniques and practices (see Chapter 6).

On an Airstream you can do your own brake adjusting easily and I assume other trailers have similar systems. Get one wheel off the ground. This is done with the dura-torque axle by pulling, or backing, the trailer so that one wheel is on a 4" block. This leaves the paired wheel (same side) clear of the pavement for ready adjustment. With a brake-adjusting tool or a bent screwdriver pry the rubber stoppers from the access hole on the drum casing (put them in your shirt pocket so you won't go off and leave them on the ground when you're finished) and, using the tool, move the drum rachet toward the center of the wheel (this movement can be determined by means of a flashlight beam directed into the aperature) until the wheel can no longer be turned by hand. Presumably this tightening operation is supposed to prepare the shoe for more uniform alignment when re-tightened. Now back the rachet off until the wheel turns freely (probably about twelve notches). There may be a slight grating at one or two points as the wheel turns but as long as there is no checking or slowing of the wheel your adjustment is complete.

Battery Maintenance

If you have the Uni-Volt charging system you will want to check your battery for over-charging anytime you connect to a new power source. As soon as your Bat-Check (battery condition meter) shows a full charge (with power switch off temporarily) remove the caps from your battery cells and see if the battery is 'gassing' (boiling off the water from the electrolyte). If it is gassing there is a strap adjustment which must be performed in order to reduce the charging rate (resulting when the input power is above 110 volts). Consult your instruction sheet for the converter to determine which terminals the strap should be moved to. The later model Airstream employs the Uni-Volt Mark III which is so designed that the adjustment is never necessary (and none is provided).

The appearance of verdegris (a greenish deposit) on battery terminals is the result of electrolysis and indicates a poor con-

MAINTENANCE AND REPAIR

nection at the terminal. The terminal lug should be removed and both the inside of the lug and the outside of the terminal post cleaned until bright. The battery post should be reshaped with a shaping tool, available in auto supply stores for a few cents, as a mishapen post will result in a poor connection and more electrolysis. This condition should be corrected as soon as it is observed as the electrolytic action eats away at the lead and causes the connection to get progressively worse. Many a new battery is sold to the unsuspecting motorist when starting trouble, dim lights, etc. develop as a result of a poor battery post connection.

Don't be tempted to file away the tips of the lug jaws when tightening the lugs as they serve to align the opposing faces of the lug for a better connection.

7-Way Plug

Aside from remembering to flush the plug and jack with dry lubricant each time you hitch up to travel, maintenance of the plug is fairly simple. The spring-loaded cover on the receptacle will keep it reasonably dry and clean, providing it has been mounted high enough on the bumper so that it will not drag on uneven terrain, and the plug should be stowed open-face down, but suspended above the ground, when you are parked, to protect it from the rain. However, if you are to park it for some time in a humid climate, or even for a few days at the seashore, it is a good idea to cover both plug and receptacle to keep out moisture.

Oven

Extended travel over rough roads will eventually loosen the screws that hold the burner bracket to the side of the oven as well as the bolts that hold the burner to the bracket. When this happens you can expect a broken pilot line as it cannot support the weight of the burner. Also, if the bolts work out before the screws do the burner may pull away from the supply orifice far enough to allow gas to accumulate in the oven and this might result in an explosion.

In my opinion this situation calls for a preventive maintenance procedure. Every five thousand miles of towing, and before lighting the oven after travelling a stretch of rough road, remove the portable cover from the burner support bracket and tighten the two bolts and the two scews.

Your oven pilot is likely to need adjusting. With both my Magic Chef ovens this was the case. The pilots were too low to hold the thermocouple open for the secondary pilot to light. In the present one, the secondary pilot (the one that lights the main burner) was too low to ignite from the primary pilot. It could be lighted separately, with a match, while the primary pilot kept the thermocouple open, but then it was so low that there was

MAINTENANCE AND REPAIR

invariably quite an explosion every time the oven came on because of the inadequate pilot flame. Primary pilot adjustment is directly behind the pilot assembly, secondary pilot behind the oven control.

Little attention seems to be given to gas appliance adjustments in general, either by the appliance company or the trailer manufacturer. However, the pilot adjusting screw in any gas appliance, if there is one, can be found simply by tracing the small gas line that leads away from it. In some cases this screw is exposed to view and can be adjusted readily; in others it may be under or behind a large flat screw which serves as a gas-tight cover over the adjusting screw.

In some appliances the pilot may need to be stronger than the "blue-tipped" flame considered most desirable in order to keep it from being blown out by wind gusts or by the terminal explosion sometimes occuring when the main burner is extinguished at the end of a heating cycle.

If you find that a pilot is too low, and can't be adjusted high enough to operate its associated themocouple or if it has no adjustment (assuming the thermocouple to be functioning — and if a higher flame will operate the thermocouple it is probably not at fault), then the orifice is probably fouled or corroded. These will usually respond to a cleaning with alcohol and air jet (soak it a few minutes then blow it out). Do **not** attempt to clean an orifice with any metal tool (pin, wire, or what have you) or you will be buying a new one.

The oven main burner will probably need the air sleeve adjusted, as will the range. Simply move the sleeve so as to increase the air volume until the flame becomes tipped with yellow, then close the opening down again until the yellow tip can just be seen occasionally.

Range

The range burners are adjusted exactly the same way as the oven burner. Sometimes it gets adjusted more frequently — For the first year of use our range gave us a lot of trouble. The burners were extremely erratic. First one and then two would produce a high yellow flame, not quite hot enough to melt butter, then a low blue one. Once in a while one of them would appear to be about right. After some months I felt sufficiently pressed to remove the cover and have a look at the air input sleeves serving the burners. None of the three were alike so I set each one for maximum blue flame (all three appeared to be exactly alike for the correct setting) and replaced the cover. The next day I found two of them acting up again so I dismissed the problem as being some sort of natural phenomenon. A few weeks later I removed the cover again to give the more inaccessible portions of the range a good cleaning (the previous removal had disclosed

MAINTENANCE AND REPAIR

that small bits of debris had collected in the corners) and promptly stumbled upon the source of trouble.

The air adjusting sleeves were no longer where I had set them. One was closed completely and two were wide open. At first I though they might have been turned by vibration but they obviously fit too snugly for that. Then it dawned on me that my wife was the culprit. In her zealous endeavor to keep the range clean she was reaching back under the cover far enough to catch her dish cloth in the sleeves and move them around. Inasmuch as she felt obliged to perform this cleaning ritual every time she washed dishes the burners couldn't be depended upon to work the same any two times in succession! Solution? A dab of epoxy on each sleeve. They haven't moved since.

Water Heater

In adjusting the pilot on the water heater high enough to withstand strong wind gusts I found that it would form a soot deposit rapidly where the tip of it contacted the top of the combustion air channel wherein the pilot was situated. By bending the pilot mounting bracket down I was able to gain sufficient clearance for a full inch of pilot flame — and with 40 to 60 knot wind gusts in the high desert, even that wouldn't always stay lighted.

The air sleeve on the water heater main burner may need adjusting, also. This should be set for enough air so that the burner doesn't give off an odor but not so much that the combustion noise is objectionable — and it can produce quite a roar if a high volume of air is admitted.

The new model Bowen with which my '68 is equipped doesn't have the pilot space problem — it is provided with practically unlimited space. And whether I'm supposed to do so or not, I've adjusted it a couple of notches high so that it will stay lighted in medium strong wind gusts and while cruising. I like to have hot water when I want it, and besides, the water heater pilot is very difficult to light in a strong breeze — in a wind, impossible. It hasn't been out for two months now, and is still going strong. However, if you are one of those who likes to shut the heater down while traveling, I suggest the use of an LP gas torch for lighting — the extra heat operates the thermocouple in a few seconds instead of several minutes, and lets you get off your heels.

Furnace

The International furnace (I think called the "Little Darling' by some) with which my '65 Airstream was equipped is, itself, a good furnace although not designed for trailer travel in subfreezing weather because it can't be persuaded to remain in

MAINTENANCE AND REPAIR

operation when travelling at normal highway speeds. But then, who is fool enough to travel in any such weather if the means is at hand to head south? Besides me, that is? However, the best of furnaces can't heat satisfactorily without proper thermostatic control. And the best thermostat produced can't control a furnace adequately if it is improperly located.

The manufacturer had chosen to locate the thermostat on my model in the bedroom, on the rear partition wall over the bed. Being so far from the principle heat source (the living room register) it lagged behind the furnace operation by 10 to 20 degrees, depending upon whether or not the bathroom door was closed (where an auxiliary register was located).

The best location, I discovered by trying several, is the face of the divan post almost directly in front of the register. Here the first flow of warm air quickly heats up the thermal element and operates the thermostat, cutting off the burner. The circulator fan continues to force heat from the already heated furnace bonnet for a moment or so and then shuts down. This anticipating of the temperature rise enables the thermostat to settle down right on temperature and provides a temperature regulation usually within one degree in the center of the living area.

I found this location effective, also, in the '67 Airstream. However, the side panels had to be removed from the new type thermostat (a one minute operation with the tin snips) in order to make it more sensitive to the horizontal flow of warm air, it having been designed for vertical flow (open at top and bottom). A readymade conduit was already in place in the '67 — the channel wherein the freeze-proof water line is run along the bottom of the wall. I simply tucked the thermostat extension wires under this channel, out of sight, connected the free ends to the previously mounted thermostat, and the job was done.

For the epitome of luxury, leave the original thermostat in the bedroom and simply connect the new one in parallel with it. Then you can switch control from one thermostat to the other, night and day, by simply turning off the one you don't want to use at the moment. There is no doubting the feeling of luxury one experiences, reaching out from under the covers to turn the thermostat up so the trailer will be warm for bathing or dressing.

Incidentally, the '68 Airstream incorporates a newer thermostat (remove the press-fit cover and find the model designation HC2 stamped on the base) that cuts the furnace off at about 63 degrees. I much prefer the '67 type as it enabled me to maintain a night time temperature of about 55 and still not run the risk of freezing the water pipes. If you are operating a '68 Airstream in sub-freezing weather be very careful how low you set the thermostat when you are away or asleep. You will detect almost imperceptible resistance to the movement of the con-

MAINTENANCE AND REPAIR

trol, from right to left, as you approach a setting of 63 degrees. Anywhere left of that point the control will shut the main burner off. Of course if the furnace manifold is hot the circulatory fan will continue to run until it cools, but that's it — no more heat until you move the control to the right of the cut-off point.

The International furnace itself gave me very little trouble except that it would occasionally put itself out by an unusually strong terminal explosion ending a heating cycle. Discussing this phenomenon with Milton Zink (on the '65 Alaska caravan) I learned that the furnace manufacturer's representative had corrected Zink's similar trouble (a '64 Airstream) by blanking off one of the air aperatures in the main burner. Upon removing the burner I found that a makeshift blank had already been installed but that it fitted very poorly. I shimmed it so that it performed its intended function, and the terminal explosions decreased in force to a slight cough — and no longer extinguished the pilot.

A few months later, in the high desert where strong wind guests were frequent, the furnace started going out again. I adjusted the pilot for maximum flame, which didn't seem to be very much, with no results. About the only way I could get the thing relighted with the wind blowing was by using my liquid gas 'Bernz-O-Matic' blow torch. Then any good strong gust would blow it out again. With the temperature at 10 to 20 degrees every night this soon proved unacceptable so I took the problem up with a trailer shop man who had had considerable experience with mobile home furnaces. At his suggestion I removed the pilot and cleaned the orifice with alcohol and forced air, and also spread the pilot side of the fan-shaped diverter that directs the pilot flame so that a somewhat larger portion of the flame struck the thermal element (the bulk of the pilot flame is directed toward the burner). It worked. With a larger flame and the flames directed more onto the element the pilot stopped going out except in the very strongest wind gusts.

I probably should relate that I had tried every conceivable kind of wind shield — rabbit ears, etc. — without any success, before cleaning the pilot.

Don't attempt to remove the burner and pilot assembly without a good ½" drive rachet, with extensions, and a 5/16" deep-throat socket, or you're sure to lose your religion. With the proper tools disassembly is tedious but simple. First remove the two nuts from the studs that hold the circulator fan in place and remove it. Then remove about twenty more similar nuts on the face plate, one that holds a positioning bracket on the gas line, and you're ready to disconnect the gas line and remove the furnace face plate to which the burner and pilot are attached. It all comes out as an integral assembly. Then disconnect the pilot gas line and proceed with cleaning the orifice.

MAINTENANCE AND REPAIR

Refrigerator

Aside from the need for a 12" by 12" air block to be placed over the floor opening when travelling, to prevent the burner from being extinguished, I know of only two minor problems encountered with the later model Dometic refrigerators. One arises from repeated use of the flint (as is likely to happen until you learn how to keep the thing on while you travel). Flint dust chokes up the orifice and has to be removed. However, cleaning is a simple procedure. Simply remove the sheet-metal cover (secured around the burner to reduce drafts), remove the burner barrel (consult the manufacturer's instructions on this procedure) and clean it with alcohol and an air jet.

The other problem arises after prolonged use of the gas refrigerating unit — and sometimes sooner if the flame is improperly adjusted or there is insufficient combustion air being admitted to the chamber. The burner flue becomes partially blocked with soot. When this occurs the special "brush" (a helically shaped strip of metal) which the manufacturer furnishes with the unit and which you will find suspended from the top, and inside, of the flue enables the flue to be cleaned with ease. Remember to cover the burner with aluminum foil, or other suitable material, before cleaning the flue. If you are sharp you will cover the area at the bottom of the flue with dampened paper towels so that the soot you dislodge can be readily removed when you've finished the job. You are sure to accumulate sufficient soot to blacken every square inch of surface inside the trailer. I know of one individual who ignored this precaution, **once,** electing to let the soot fall where it would and then to whiff it up with a vacuum cleaner. It worked beautifully, but the vacuum cleaner had to be retired, even after several cleanings — little black smudges continued to appear out of nowhere, just like magic. I'm convinced that an ounce of this material would, with a suitable vehicle, paint the city of New York a beautiful black black.

Electric Wiring

Wiring connections sometimes work loose. And although loose connections in low voltage systems rarely cause fires, other problems are generated — and once in a great while the exception occurs and we do have a fire. However, loose connections can be very annoying, and sometimes expensive.

For example, a loose terminal lug in the furnace circuit can drop the voltage at the motor terminals sufficiently to cause the motor to run so slow that it will draw too much current (insufficent counter electromotive force developed — for you engineer types) and result in a tripped circuit breaker. Incidentally, anytime electrical trouble of any kind is encountered, all **connec**tions in the circuit should be tightened before defective com-

MAINTENANCE AND REPAIR

ponents are suspected. This is analogous to making sure all the stop cocks and valves are open in a water supply system before ordering a new pump.

Summary

You must have concluded by this time that you've got to be a jack of all trades — that is, if you are going to get anything like continuous service out of your trailer. With all the extra conveniences and special comfort systems which are incorporated in the better quality travel trailers — and in view of the rigorous treatment they receive in normal use — troubles are bound to develop. Your salvation is to learn all you can about your trailer, through the Owner's Manual (Airstream now provides an excellent one), rally maintenance bull-sessions, caravan trouble discussions and tips you pick up from fellow trailerists. Also, whenever you take your trailer in for repairs, factory, dealer or appliance shop — insist on your right to watch them perform the repair work. You will no doubt need to do that very same work sooner or later and a little kibitzing now may save you many hours later. Some factories refuse to allow their customers into their repair shops to watch work performed on their own trailers. The manufacturer who follows this policy is pretty short-sighted, or benighted. We who have been trailering for some time can tell him that every thing each customer learns about repairing his unit will save the manufacturer both in shop time on warranty (whether it be in the factory or at a certified service center shop) as well as improve his image with his customers, because that knowledge will be passed on to many more owners of the same brand trailer, at rallys, parks, and other places, and used many times over. Any repair outfit that wants to hide its work from the customer is not to be trusted, anyway. I'm forced to recall the article published in Reader's Digest some years back, disclosing that a big proportion of garages who hid their work from the customer employed incompetent mechanics or were out to cheat the customer by charging for work not done and parts not used. For example, if both warranty work and non-warranty work were both in progress on your trailer it would be pretty simple for all the labor to be charged to your non-warranty work, wouldn't it? But not if you're working with them. Insist on it.

If you prove to be too much of a burden (argumentative, demanding, abusive, obstructive, etc.) any self-respecting shop superintendent will promptly ask you to take your trailer somewhere else — as he will have a perfect right to do. Of course the manufacturer's shop work will slow down — so what? He will reap a harvest of subsequent repair work saved many times that originally expended. The reward for the private repair outfit lies in the increased referrals and repeat customers he is bound to harvest. Of further value, if given an opportunity, **many customers are capable of contributing measurably to the efficiency of shop**

MAINTENANCE AND REPAIR

work — both by experienced suggestion and by participation in the work.

Tool List and Equipment List

The tools and equipment required to perform most of the routine maintenance and repairs to your car and trailer, as well as the alterations you may undertake are listed below. It is suggested that you buy only good quality tools — cheap tools lend a false sense of security and then fail you at the crucial moment.

If you have no mechanical capability and have no wish to acquire any you will have no use for these tools, unless perhaps you might seek help from someone who has — and you could at least supply the tools. If this latter description fits you it might be well for you to stay pretty close to repair facilities or to travel in company any time you take to the wilderness.

Two advantages afforded by tools, and the ability to use them, are convenience and economy. At $6.00 an hour (and up) for mechanical work, however simple, you can pay for your tools in short order — from then on your use of them is pure profit. And, by effecting an occasional simple repair yourself you can keep travelling on your way, without the inconvenience of a day or two at a repair shop. Don't forget to obtain a shop manual for your car from the manufacturer. When you are off the beaten path it's an indispensible aid.

Tool List

common plier (2 pairs)
long-nose pliers
diagonal pliers
wide-grip pliers
vice-grip pliers
3/8" screw driver
1/4" screw driver, short
1/4" screw driver, long
Medium phillips-head screw driver
Set of Allen Wrenches
Set of 1/4" drive deep-throat sockets with extensions and rachet
Set of 3/8" drive sockets with universal and rachet
8" mill file
8" round file
claw hammer
rubber hammer, 16 oz.
pop rivet gun
pop-rivets, short, medium and long
hack saw with blades for steel & copper
coping saw
set ignition wrenches

spark plug wrench to fit 3/8" drive
7/8 open end wrench paired with 3/4
5/8 paired with 11/16 (both open end and box)
3/8 paired with 7/16 (both open end and box)
1/2 paired with 9/16 (both open end and box)
6" adjustable wrench
10" adjustable wrench
1/4" electric drill, light duty, with 3/32, 1/8, 5/32, 3/16 and 1/4 hi-speed drills
tin shears
10" pipe wrench
4" dreft
6" cold chisel, 1/2" blade
hose-clamp tool (for spring-type clamp)
Lug wrench, long handle type
Single-blade axe
hatchet
pry-bar
feeler gauge

101

MAINTENANCE AND REPAIR

Equipment List

Benz-O-Matic blow torch
Resin-core solder
masking tape, 1½"
rubber tape, electric
friction tape
2-cell or 3-cell flashlight
Portable flood lite, dry battery
Battery starting jumper cables (best)
Ball of white cord
Round point, short handled shovel
CRC 5-45 or Elmer's Glide-All
Small can (squirt type) machine oil
small squirt can 20 wt motor oil
small squirt can liquid wrench
small can Automotive Multi-purpose Grease
hitch-ball lubricant
pressure can of rust inhibiting aluminum (metal) paint
4/0 sand paper
4/0 emery cloth
wire brush
compression air pump with gauge spark plug type); available at Sears or Wards
Nylon tow line with sister-hooks attached
First-aid Kit with Red-Cross booklet
Small plastic funnel
Medium tin funnel
12-volt hand vacuum cleaner
Tire gauge, to 50 PSI

Chapter 8
TOWING OVER UNPAVED ROADS

There are a number of fundamental differences in operating your unit over unpaved roads. I think a good place to start the treatment of this subject is with the Alaska Highway through Canada (sometimes referred to as "the Alcan Highway") as it is probably the longest uninterrupted stretch of unpaved road to be encountered anywhere in North America — approximately 1100 miles from where the asphalt terminates 86.3 miles north of Dawson Creek, British Columbia, and where it begins at the Alaskan border.

We travelled this road in the summer of 1965 with a large group of Airstream trailers in caravan. Naturally, the recommendations offered here were developed from the experiences of various members of the caravan, including my own, plus information garnered along the way from service and supply points.

In order to travel this road economically, comfortably and with maximum safety, your tow vehicle and your driving will require some refurbishing. Nothing difficult or expensive — but quite essential. The roughness of the road surface (at times), the loose gravel and the dust combine to force the traveller to compensate for them — or else.

The most important item in checking your car for this trip is tire quality. Even with 400 pounds more weight on the rear axle than on the front we reduced new all-weather tread on the rear by more than half in approximately 3,500 miles of gravel surfaced road and 2,000 miles of asphalt (shot treatment) paving. With proper driving at moderate speeds a set of new tires on the rear, good tires on trailer and the car front, and a spare fo each vehicle will see you through. Tire repair facilities are frequent and new tires are available at most. Remember that, in an emergency, any tire that has your rim size still serve.

If there is any question of your car's ability to travel the distance, each way, then you will do well to take along a few spares. Among the most common failures are plugs, points and condenser, coil, fuel filter, fuel pump, hoses (including power equipment hoses), drive belts, generator or alternator and regulator. If each of these items is relatively new you should have no trouble.

TOWING OVER UNPAVED ROADS

For the most up-to-date information on repair facilities on the highway, as well as data on outstanding sights and other pertinent information, you may obtain a copy of the most recent issue of "The Milepost" at practically any service station along the way. This is a most excellent guide book and is carried by almost every one who travels the Alaska Highway.

The mechanical preparation of your trailer will also need some looking into. Your 6-way electric circuit connector should be in first class condition — a spare may be in order. Wheel bearings should be greased if they are scheduled within the next five thousand miles or if they have not been serviced since purchasing the trailer.

Both car and trailer will need some protection from flying gravel and other road hazards, and your trailer will want "dust-proofing." First let's take a look at the car. You can protect your gas tank from damage by having your dealer put on an extra heavy coat of standard undercoating. One-eighth inch will do. A rubber or fabric over is not necessary if so protected, and actually may cause a leak by trapping stones between cover and tank and wearing through. A major repair facility in Dawson Creek reported that at least one-fourth of the tanks coming to them for repair are ruptured in this manner.

Heavy rubber gravel shields mounted behind your own rear tires will reduce bombardment of the front of your trailer, as well as the possibility of damage to your car's fenders and tail skirt.

A "bug-shield" mounted up front, large enough to project at least 4" above the level of your hood and extend from side to side (and preferably a little over on the left) will protect your radiator, front trim and paint, and windshield, not only from bug nuisance but, of more importance, from gravel damage. You've a good chance of suffering a windshield replacement anyway, but most comprehensive policies cover this loss.

For the trailer, the first and most important consideration is to protect the front from flying gravel. Otherwise, you are almost certain to suffer a broken window and the lower front will be thoroughly "embossed" if not ruined. After observing many varieties of protective shields or guards utilized by caravan members and noting the results of each I recommend a 4 ft. by 8 ft. sheet of ¼" exterior grade plywood or thin masonite wrapped around the front end of the trailer and projecting 4" below the bottom envelope. This should render most gravel harmless, whether thrown by your own wheels or by those of other vehicles. Do **not** follow some well-intentioned advice to secure the gravel shield with any kind of adhesive tape (masking, dust, or otherwise) or you will have a post-trip problem trying to get it off. Use pop-rivets, 24" on center and follow the seams. You can always drill them out and install new ones when you re-

TOWING OVER UNPAVED ROADS

"A furnace filter secured in place of the front window sceen keeps dust out while allowing open window to build up pressure inside trailer and eliminate dust being vacuumed into trailer from the underside. A sheet of heavy, corrugated, plastic will prevent damage to the front of the trailer. For heavy-footed drivers a 4 ft. by 8 ft. sheet of masonite or plywood is surer."

move the shield, with only minor disturbance of the exterior appearance of your trailer.

Gas lines, as well as any exposed wiring under the trailer, must be protected. Most of us used 5/8" water hose, split on a spiral, for covering these items.

For keeping the dust out of your trailer (and this is a must unless you want to breathe dust, eat dust, and wear dust) an air intake filter proved to be the only effective solution. However, the installation has to suit the aerodynamics of the tow vehicle. For sedans and convertibles, a pair of 16" by 25" disposable-type furnace filters (doubled), fitted to the front window opening (most of us simply utilized a sheet of plywood cut to replace the window screen, with a 15" x 24" aperature) with the bottom of the window cranked open about 12" will prove quite effective. The air pressure thus developed inside the trailer keeps the dust out. For station-wagon and truck or camper types this location proved generally ineffective, apparently because of the volume of dust drawn into the space between vehicles by

TOWING OVER UNPAVED ROADS

venturi action of the rear of the vehicle. With these latter vehicles the best solution seems to be filters placed in the forward overhead vent with the vent opened at the front only. There were one or two instances of damaged vents when these vehicles were operated above 40 MPH. Although not nearly as effective as the front window treatment, the overhead vent reduced the volume of dust considerably.

Protect your front window with a sheet of any semi-rigid material (plywood, plexi-glass, rock-shield, masonite, etc. I heard of only two instances of broken side windows but you might carry along a 50c piece of oil-cloth for covering the opening in the event you do lose one until you get where you can have the frame reglazed.

Unless you have been on gravel roads for extended distances before with your trailer you can profit from some of the driving principles we developed on the trip. Conditions vary according to class of material found locally available by the road crews as well as current weather conditions and maintenance work load. After weeks of dry weather the surface is mostly loose gravel over hardpacked base. After good, soaking rains the graders provide a surface which rivals asphalt or pavement except for occasional chug-holes. When there is loose gravel there is also unusually rough surface, with many small chug holes. Either they, or the loose gravel, is sufficient reason for proceeding slowly (25 to 45 MPH, generally). It's the speed of the vehicle intercepting the missile that makes the dents and breaks the glass. A good practice is to slow down when meeting or being passed, especially if you are on the outside of a curve or if there is loose gravel on the surface.

Water is no problem. With the exception of the first two hundred miles or so beyond Ft. St. John service stations are prepared to furnish the customers water in exchange for their trade. I found it a good practice to state my need for "gas **and** water" and inquire about the availability and quality of water before procuring gas. If you stop while you still have half a tank or so of gas you can take your business on up the highway if no water is forthcoming. Here the Milepost can serve as your guide as it lists all service stations, giving milepost location and brand of gas dispensed.

Parking will be the least of your problems. Throughout the length of the highway, and all through Alaska, we found government campgrounds, at no charge, located at frequent intervals. The Milepost will list those on these highways. There are many other parking places suitable for parking as long as you are equipped with utilities.

Shorter trips over unpaved roads require only as much of the heretofore described preparation and precaution as you may care to indulge. For a distance of only a few miles I would suggest

TOWING OVER UNPAVED ROADS

that you open the front window of the trailer (or overhead vent, according to type of tow vehicle) to keep out your own (vacuum created) dust, and drive on **slowly.** Slow driving will avoid damage from gravel thrown by your own tires and the only dust that will enter the trailer will be that which is 'scooped' in by the opening in the window as you meet other vehicles.

Chapter 9
HOUSEKEEPING HINTS

There are as many ways to do trailer housekeeping as there are trailerists. Each person develops his own special ways. But just to get you started in the right direction here are a few hints.

Stowage

Much more safe, secure and convenient storage can be realized by the use of various sizes and shapes of plastic containers. My wife used about four dozen of these, each one especially selected to accommodate one or a group of items. The method is safer because spillage is greatly reduced by providing a snug fit in each container and if it does spill the contents are confined to the plastic container. Secure, because items can be fitted neatly together for less movement. Convenient, because each container (tray, jar, cannister, bin, etc.) can be readily lifted out onto a working surface to enable ready selection of the desired item without the necessity of standing on one's head while reaching.

Holding Tank or 'Sanitator'

Owners' manuals usually carry pretty complete instructions on the use of this convenience. But in case you've bought a used trailer and no manual was provided you will want to know that no paper other than white toilet tissue should be placed in it, that only especially prepared cleaning agents (such as TST or Pink Magic) should ever be used (detergents and soaps tend to corrode the gate valves and mechanisms and render them inoperative after a while) and that the tank should not be used as a 'thru line' to the sewer but should be used as a tank until half full or better and then dumped. Otherwise the gate valve is likely to become clogged with undissolved paper remnants and you will have a real problem. See Chapter 5 for a more detailed treatment of this item.

HOUSEKEEPING HINTS

"Selected sizes of plastic containers triple the effective capacity of the refrigerator, and make removal of foods easy."

HOUSEKEEPING HINTS

Water Supply

As long as you travel in the U.S. and get your supply from sources of approved city water you don't have to be concerned. When travelling we fill up once a day when we stop for gas. Incidentally, if your tank does not have an air vent you will want to install one; service station operators are loath to have you block a complete drive-thru (and two to six tanks) while you dribble water into your tank — and that is about the rate at which an unvented tank will accept water. Some are equipped with it when they come from the factory and some are not. I can't figure this one out — unless one man is assigned to the task on an assembly line and he takes a lot of coffee breaks. If you have the capability for filling your tank at the higher rate insist on using the car-wash hose rather than the radiator filling hose — or you may still be fifteen minutes at the task, instead of three or four.

However, you may occasionally have to resort to untested well water, or even water from a stream. Or you may travel in Mexico where virus to which we Americanos are susceptible are said to abound in the water. In these cases it is recommended that all water be either boiled or treated. The Chlorox we purchased near the Mexican border carried instructions to add one ounce to each thirty gallons of suspected water, and then allow several hours for the purification process before using. Our procedure included the foregoing precaution, except that we doubled the amount of Chlorox recommended. We bought only bottled water from city suppliers and to each tank full we added two ounces of Chlorox. We used this water for washing everything that was handled by native hands — vegetables, fruits, food cans, bottles, bread wrappers, etc. before stowing it away for future use. And water used for cooking or for brushing teeth was drawn through the purifier, in addition. The people with whom we came in contact in Mexico were every bit as clean as Americans — but they wash with Mexico's water, and we are cautioned repeatedly that virus strains are there. And we do know there are many, many northern citizens who contract the virus, commonly termed as "touriste" or "Montezuma's Revenge". Some say that it isn't the water at all, that it is in the air, or that it's their highly spiced food. Anyway, we always take the foregoing precautions — and the Entero Talidina which we bought to take along on the first trip is still in the medicine chest — unopened. Of course, when we eat out we eat only freshly cooked food and drink only bottled beverages, and only at the better hotels and restaurants catering to Americans or Europeans.

Cold Beds

Due to the minimum of insulation over the wheel wells (I personally watched a factory hand split a 2½" bat down the

HOUSEKEEPING HINTS

middle and put the half-thick batt over the wheel well) beds that are placed here have a tendency to be very cold. If you don't use your trailer in cold weather you need not be concerned. But when the temperature drops the cold is relatively unimpeded in its progress through the under shell and it penetrates all the way through the mattress. So, even though the inside of the trailer may be kept at 70 degrees all day, the mattress, having been shielded from the interior warmth by the cover (the more blankets in place, the worse the condition) is thoroughly chilled — so much so that when you retire the mattress continues to draw the heat out of your body for hours. Twin bed models are twice as bothersome in this category as are doubles because the double bed spreads the cold from one wheel well over twice the area.

Double bed models with the pull-out type bed are even less bothered because the divan back is on edge all day, soaking up warmth from the trailer's heated air, and the divan seat, as soon as it is pulled out into sleeping position, has its underside exposed to the trailer's warmth. Further, neither seat nor back are covered all day long so they have at least an even chance of staying warm. Obviously, then, for cold weather use you'd do better with a pull-out bed model.

The manufacturer needs to give this area maximum attention. Airstream has obviously recognized the problem — my '68 has the bed elevated, with plenty of room for insulation between the inner and outer liners over the wheel wells. Also the new Urethane foam type insulation is used exclusively over the entire underside of the primary floor (between that and the underbody sheath). The improvement over the old method is remarkable.

Sliding Drapes

Many travel trailers employ drapes that are attached to runners at top or at both top and bottom. You can save your epithets if you will take the trouble to apply some of the new Slipicone lubricant to the plastic sliders or to the slotted hanger in which they slide. After treating my new ones they can be opened or closed fully with a flick of the wrist.

Sliding Drawers and Pull-out Beds

The same lubricant applied to bed runners and to drawer runners make them a delight to operate. A few ounces of pressure will move any drawer in or out. The pull-out beds can be handled by a child. Don't know why they didn't have the stuff the first couple of years I trailered!

Carpeting

A good grade of carpeting can be installed in your trailer for a few dollars, and this feature offers a number of advantages. The floor, hence the trailer, remains warmer in cold weather.

HOUSEKEEPING HINTS

Everything in the trailer collects less dust as any dust brought in on shoes is promptly collected by the carpet, to be sucked into the vacuum cleaner at the daily cleaning (the new 12-volt portables make this by far the easiest way to sweep — and you don't sweep dust all over everything as you do with a broom). A word of caution — select a mottled pattern so that water spots, generated while serving table, doing dishes, etc. won't show. Otherwise be prepared to use rug runners between the range and the dining table, and at the entrance.

Overhead Vents

The better quality roof vents utilize a thick (approximately 7" soft foam gasket. The vent cover should not be drawn down tightly against these gaskets as they will last much, much longer — and function just as well — if the cover is drawn down only until the gasket begins to compress.

Windows

In extremely hot weather window frames have a tendency to stick to the rubber weather stripping. Again our old friend, Mr. Slipicone, will remove the problem.

Chapter 10
GETTING THE MOST FROM YOUR TRAILER

Among the factors that provide for using your trailer to the best possible advantage, to you and to others, are economy, convenience, safety (both from hazard and from molestation) and freedom from repressive regulations.

These factors suggest a number of rules which many trailerists have learned to observe in order to realize their maximum advantages and to perpetuate those that are subject to deterioration by regulations which can be imposed by various authorities such as local administrations, police and highway departments, recreational park authorities and by individual property owners. It is realized that these rules are, in some instances, covered in detail in the foregoing chapters. However, on this subject a little repetition may not be remiss. There are always exceptions to any rule, of course, but the following list will serve you and your fellow trailerists to good advantage if observed faithfully:

1. Drive at least twenty percent slower than the posted speed limit, and never over 50 MPH except in emergency or when absolutely necessary. It's safer, for you and others on the highway; it gives you a chance to enjoy the scenery; it's more restful; it takes less gas and reduces the wear and tear on both vehicles tremendously.

2. Avoid driving in or near cities during rush hours when practicable. You can pretty well manage this by varying your daily departure and stopping times to suit.

3. For overnight stops (assuming you are self-contained) take advantage of roadside rests and parks, state and national recreation facilities (the Federal Recreation Area Entrance Permit, at $7.00, provides a tremendous bargain if you travel quite a bit) and, in fact, any public area where overnight stops are permitted. In most western states on both federal and state highways there is usually ample parking area on the right-of-way, far enough from the roadway to escape, to a large degree, the rush and noise of passing vehicles. Our favorite practice, when travelling in the

GETTING THE MOST

Many states provide attractive rest stops, suitable for meal-time or over-night. This one, on a state route in Georgia, is typical. Members of trailering fraternities habitually leave such sites cleaner than they find them, picking up the previous user's rubbish if he left any.

west, is to turn off onto a side road a few hundred feet to get away from the traffic noise. The only western states which have antequated laws prohibiting overnight stops are California and Wyoming. However almost all states prohibit overnight stops in some roadside parks or rests, usually at or near a town or city, but in such cases the area is clearly posted. Washington prohibits overnight stops in all roadside rests but permits it off the open highway.

Other than in the west, Illinois, Indiana, Connecticut, Ohio, New York and Wisconsin prohibit while all others permit or leave it up to local authorities — in which event if it's banned it will be posted. In the more heavily populated areas, or in high agricultural land use areas, there is seldom suitable parking space anyway so the question becomes largely academic. Which same probably accounts for the fact that there is ten times as much travel, by trailers, in the west. Who wants to search out a trailer park (assuming space is available) and go to all that trouble of hooking up, anyway?

When stopping at night, keep a battery-powered spot-light and a firearm handy and the door locked. Keep the drapes se-

GETTING THE MOST

curely closed, even when lights are out — don't give a would-be hijacker a chance to size up the lay-out. Don't unlock the door for anyone until you have assured yourself beyond any doubt that it can be done with complete safety (My Airstream has a floodlight near the door that helps out tremendously here). Don't even open for the law (you can demand that a warrant be produced, you know) unless you can see not only the uniform and badge but also the patrol car. Posing as a law officer is a favorite trick of hijackers used to gain admittance. (You see I read the Washington, D.C. papers.)

Actually, I'm sure that the chances of you being molested are something like one in a million — but who wants to be the lone statistic? Besides, the feeling of security a little preparedness can give you is well worth the trouble — you'll sleep better. And if you make a habit of keeping your rock shield down over your front window — cut an aperature in it so you can observe anyone molesting your tow vehicle without opening the door and thus giving up your advantage.

5. Deposit all trash in receptacles provided. No matter how isolated you are, keep that garbage and refuse with you until you pass a litter barrel or until you are in a facility where trash receptacles are provided (or bury it — deep). In view of our position, somewhat on the 'fringe' of society, it is especially incumbent upon us trailerists to be meticulous in our conduct. We are being accepted more and more as a fundamental, and important, segment of American life and are accordingly treated with increasing respect. Let's do everything we can to improve our image and keep up the progress.

6. Never let your drain water run out onto the street or onto any parking area which may be used by others, whether paved or unpaved. No one wants to walk around in your dish water. Either use a bucket and carry the water to a sump or to a suitable sand, brush or weed patch where it can be properly disposed of, or provide yourself with a water hose fitting on your drain so that each time you stop you can connect a drain hose and carry the end off to a suitable drain area.

I have observed that, in many parks, buckets are required under the drain in trailer parking areas but not in camping areas, where the drain hose can be used. In most cases trailers are permitted in camping areas, and I find campgrounds generally more to my liking, anyway. Besides, there is sometimes an extra charge for using trailer parking — with a self contained unit who needs one? Except every week or so if no dumping station is handy? The new Thetford water saver with the 20 gallon tank in the Airstream is good for two to three weeks.

7. Learn to stow your refrigerator in the most efficient manner possible and keep a good stock of fresh fruits, vegetables, meats and dairy products. There is no excuse for eating poorly

GETTING THE MOST

when travelling with a self-contained unit. By using selected sizes of plastic trays of varying depth we can put just about four cubic feet of food in our four cubic foot box — a full week's suply of fresh foods — and frequently do.

8. Eat properly. Take the time to stop at meal times where you can prepare and eat a good meal. Take a nap if you feel like it. I think it was Mark Twain who said "Nothing improves on good scenery more than a full stomach and the sense of well being that it brings." Partake of a light evening meal so that you can turn in early and be up and on the road when travelling is at its best.

9. Take your trailer with you — to the Rockies, the Badlands, the deserts and the snows, assuming that you have the minmum power to weight ratio discussed in an earlier chapter, of course. This power ratio, as embodied in my Imperial/Overlander rig (11,600 lbs. gross) has demonstrated its capability by traversing all U.S. highway grades in the Rockies, California 39 from Azusa to Big Pines, California 18 from Luscerne to Big Bear, Utah's access road to Canyonlands National Park and Dead Horse Point state park, access road to Chisos Basin in Great Bend National Park and from there to Presidio over Texas 170. These registered from 17% to 30% grade on my inclinometer, the Utah grade capping the lot at 30%.

However, it is a good idea to stay off dead end roads. Remember that your turning radius constitutes the smallest area in which you can turn your rig.

10. See your national parks and monuments. We have learned that each and every one of them offers a rewarding experience. Many state parks are equally good — but usually somewhat more expensive.

11. Refrain from cutting or trimming natural growth and from collecting rocks and minerals unless you have received express permission to do so. Every act of destructive nature however small in your estimation, and this includes items 5 and 6, contributes to the need for repressive regulations. If depradations are observed, authorities soon add another restriction in an attempt to curtail them.

One of the areas among the tamarask groves in Death Valley, previously open to campers, is now reported closed because people continued to "trim" the branches in order to park their rigs further under the shade. Soon, with each camper taking his little twig or branch here and there, the grove began to look like a blight had struck it. Signs posted throughout the area, prohibiting the disturbance of natural growth, were ignored by the few to the detriment of many.

12. GO WEST! Go west, where natures geological wonders are laid bare and scenic vistas are vast and colorful; where the travel trailer is welcome, and not just tolerated; where there is

GETTING THE MOST

ample room for stopping, day or night, and luxurious accommodations at travel trailer parks are urged on you if you want them; where space abounds, and you can drive for hours, surrounded by colorful buttes and cliffs or heavily forrested slopes and flowing rivers — and never see another car or trailer; where the next person you meet is likely to be just like you — bent on relaxation and enjoyment surrounded by beauty and quiet and open space.

Not even autumn in New England is reward enough to justify travelling the hundreds of miles of highway thru flat plains and monotonous green or brown and enduring the continuous turmoil of heavy traffic and people in a hurry. It is said that living is "being aware" of the world around you — and I'm sure that doesn't mean while ninety-nine percent of your awareness has to be devoted to keeping out of the way of jockeying traffic and rushing crowds.

Of course you can find some of the same in the cities of the west, but even in Los Angeles or San Francisco you can drive for less than an hour and find the space and quiet and horizons you need to enable you to become "aware" of the world around you.

Any awning you select should be easy to put up and to take down — otherwise you will soon tire of it and it will remain stowed most of the time. Here is one, made by Henry Duda of 3357 North Newland Avenue, Chicago that goes up — or down — in considerably less than a minute. It is called the "Zip-Dee" awning.

GETTING THE MOST

A flag pole mount permitting three flags to be flown (usually the U.S. flag, the trailer enthusiast's state flag and his host state's flag) constructed quite simply of 1½" pipe, cut on a bias and welded to the trailer jack. Note the 12v electric jacking motor mounted on top of the jack shaft in lieu of the usual hand crank.

PB-8023-6-SB
75-46T
C
B/T